Pondicherry, that was Once French India

*This book is dedicated
to the memory of my friends
Jean-Pierre Spielmann (1957-2014)
and Ajit Koujalgi (1948-2014)*

Raphaël Malangin

Pondicherry, that was Once French India

Lustre Press
Roli Books

Contents

Left:
Engraved steel plate in Sanskrit, 15th century.

Above:
Frontispiece of *Histoire des Indes Orientales* by Abbé Guyon.

Right:
Bronze of Parvati, Shiva's consort (from the Indian pantheon, Shiva is the Lord of Time), 15th century.

Introduction

In 1744, Abbé Guyon declared in the introduction to his *L'histoire des Indes Orientales*, 'There has not been a kingdom more famous, more admired by the Ancients than that of the East Indies, and at the same time less known.' From Herodotus to Marco Polo, more than ten centuries of legends and dreams were woven together, linking the development of Western civilisation with a veritable fascination for India. For France, as for the other countries of the medieval West, India was a rich source of all things exotic. In a world of symbols and signs, this wealth could lead to but one conclusion: this had to be a country quite unlike any other; and for the rare Christian travellers who reached its shores, it did indeed prove thus. They brought back tales of fabulous sights, mythological animals and descriptions of strange peoples.

From medieval times onwards the European debt to India grew exponentially. Beginning with Indian spices, which played as important a part in preparing food as they did in medieval medicine. 'As dear as pepper', was a common saying in those times; the price of Indian pepper was, in fact, close to that of gold. The aristocracy and emerging bourgeoisie were also fond of rich imported fabrics, especially Indian and Chinese silk. Marco Polo highlighted the abundance of precious stones on the Coromandel Coast; these were transported overland and thus filled the coffers of the middlemen, the Arabs, and the great trading cities, such as Venice and Genoa. It was their monopoly of this commerce that gave these Italian cities power and predominance, preparing the ground for the Renaissance and allowing well-known families of merchant bankers, such as the Medici of Florence, to forge alliances with the great European monarchies. But there was more for the path of pilgrims rarely strays too far from the routes of major commerce. India found its place in the very heart of Western culture. For the Church, India was where the Garden of Eden or even Hell might have been situated and it was recognised as one of its oldest centres for evangelism.

Pondicherry was already a town in the fourteenth century, and in all likelihood, a very sizable one, even if few traces of it remain today. Inscriptions, however, tell us about a certain Olukarai, whose name is commemorated in the town of Oulgaret. Some five or six kilometres in circumference, this medieval Indian town had a seaport suburb, known as the new settlement or '*Puducceri*' in Tamil. There is no doubt that long before the arrival of the Europeans, the town was conducting significant trade, both locally (with rural markets collecting fruit, vegetables and pottery from the surrounding areas), and regionally (importing rice from Bengal and exporting copper, tin, zinc, spices and cotton on small coastal vessels).

Like other Coromandel ports, Puducceri was particularly open to an extensive trade with Asia. Commercial relations with China, Malaysia, Pegu, Persia, Arabia and Africa, Sindh and the Molucca islands are in evidence all along the Coromandel coast. Puducceri had probably enjoyed prosperity long before the French arrived, with its entrepot trade in cotton, agricultural products, steel and iron, and its imports of silk, gold and silver from China, horses from Arabia, and spices from the Moluccas. In fact, Pondicherry has a long history of involvement in important commercial routes. In the second century BC, the Greek geographer, Ptolemy, referred to a port called Podouké on the Coromandel coast. In more recent times, this port has been identified by the archaeologist and historian, Gabriel Jouveau-Dubreuil, as the modern town of Veerampattinam, also known as Arikamedu. It was here that a Roman emporium was discovered on the banks of the Ariancoupam river, which carried on its trading activities for several centuries. It is presumed that this settlement disappeared due to flooding of the river. At the moment, very little is known about the connection between ancient and medieval Pondicherry, apart from geographical and linguistic links.

In the West, the primary preoccupation at the end of the Middle Ages was to find a way of directly controlling the route to this Indian El Dorado, a route strongly guarded by the Ottoman Turks who, led by Mahomet II, had conquered Constantinople in 1453. Two of the least favoured but also the most adventurous nations at the end of the fifteenth century – Spain of the Reconquista and Portugal – led expeditions to find the maritime route to India and China. And thus Christopher Columbus reached America and Vasco da Gama dropped anchor at Calicut in 1498, having weathered the Cape of Good Hope. He writes: 'Having discovered the country we were looking for, not to mention the spices and precious stones, it was now time to return. We set sail towards Portugal, extremely satisfied with our good fortune, which had allowed us to make such an important discovery.'

The first Western empire in India would thus be Portuguese. It was made up of a few fixed points of commerce known as trading posts, notably Calicut, Goa, Cochin and Porto Novo. But the other European nations were not to be outdone, as they could not tolerate for long the monopoly over Indian wealth enjoyed by Catholic nations such as Spain and Portugal. And so Protestant England, Holland, Denmark – all maritime countries – would send expeditions to India in the sixteenth century.

The Protestants preferred entrusting the task of sending expeditions to private individuals and formed commercial companies to finance these ventures that lasted an average of two years, and required some ten ships and several hundred men. The British East India Company was founded in 1600, and, the Dutch Vereenigde Ooste Indische Compagnie (VOC) followed in 1602. Among the first business outposts of the British were Bombay, Calcutta and Madras, while the Dutch set up shop in Pulicat and Masulipatnam. On the whole the newly arrived foreigners were received favourably by the locals, as the former brought with them a number of manufactured products, weapons of good quality, and precious metals. In addition, these foreigners took back swathes of locally produced cotton cloth to Europe, demand for which was rapidly expanding. Their arrival was also made easier by the prevailing political situation in the peninsula. Akbar's Mughal empire in North India, well organised but vast, had allowed looser and quasi-independent regional powers to emerge in South India. These '*Nawabs*', who profited from trade to considerably increase their wealth, joined in the struggle between European nations for control of the trading posts. Alliances with local powers and the course of wars in Europe meant that Cochin, for example, passed from the Portuguese to the Dutch, and then from the Dutch to the British.

The newcomers came also to Pondicherry, which was the main port for the kingdom of Gingee in the sixteenth and seventeenth centuries, and was protected by Fort Valdaour. Documents reveal the Portuguese from Porto Novo were not infrequent visitors from 1553 onwards. In 1618, they were replaced by the Dutch from Goudelour (Cuddalore), but this was only a temporary incursion as the latter moved out in 1620. Pondicherry, however, continued to attract considerable interest and was visited also by the Danes from Tranquebar. A 'Danish house' was established in Pondicherry, probably in 1624, and the Danes would remain for thirty years, marking the first European presence of any significance. However, the clouds of war were gathering over India. In order to reassert his authority in the Deccan and the southern part of India the Mughal emperor, Shah Jahan, decided to make the sultans of Bijapur and Golconda submit to his sovereignty; eventually Golconda accepted but Bijapur resisted. In the space of a few years, three Mughal armies plundered South India. The situation was summed up by a British company agent: 'Cloth is very expensive and scarce in these areas. This is due to the number of buyers, the dearth of weavers and painters, and the ruin of the country by war and famine, and also due to the fact that the two foreign countries situated at two days' walking distance from one another, are wreaking havoc in the region. The forays and pillaging by the Moors of Golconda and of Bijapur have devastated the country around the three principal ports exporting textiles, Tevenapatnam, Porto Novo and Pondicherry, the last two having been completely destroyed.' The Danes left Pondicherry in about 1656, leaving behind a region in shambles and in dire need of economic revival.

Meanwhile, in late sixteenth century Europe, France alone remained aloof from this rush toward the East Indies. This is understandable, given the time needed to consolidate the French kingdom, principally because of religious strife between Protestants and Catholics, and the Spanish predominance on the international scene. This did not prevent Jacques Cartier from exploring the Saint Lawrence river and founding Quebec in 1534. However, it was not until 1630 and the reign of Louis XIII with his minister Richelieu, that France returned to the European stage, where it would continue to be a major power until the middle of the eighteenth century.

It must be noted that in 1630, France did not yet have a navy. Richelieu knew that the country's power would be short-lived if it had no access to the Americas and India. His first decisions were to build a fleet and to found the first merchant companies. The creation of the royal navy continued under Louis XIV, but the merchant companies eventually failed. It was on Colbert's initiative that the Compagnie des Indes Orientales was created in 1664 and the first major French expeditions set sail for India. Colbert chose to entrust this work, fifteen years before the revocation of the Edict of Nantes, to a Protestant named François Caron from the Dutch company.

The French settlements, called *loges*, were temporary; they were, in fact, quarters in the town or some houses in a big Indian town where trading was permitted. The city of Surat in 1668 was the oldest and was quickly followed by Masulipatnam in 1669 and then Pondicherry.

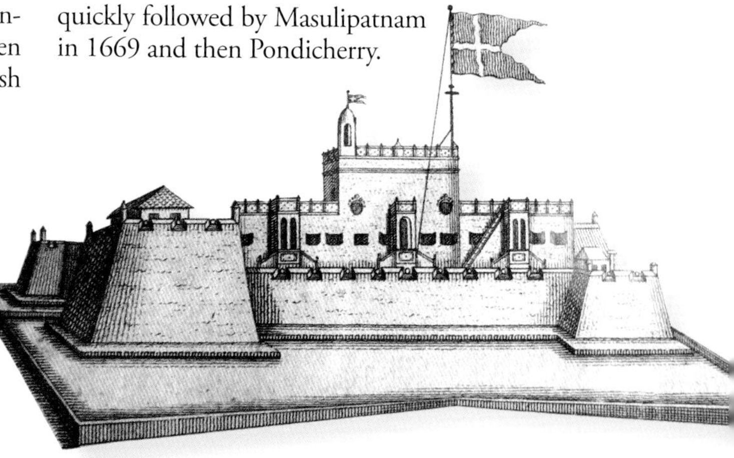

Right: Danish fort, Dansborg, at Tranquebar in the 17th century.

Top: Dutch map of South Asia, mid-17th century.

Middle: French publication of the *Recueil des Voyages* (Travel Memoirs) which was useful as a guide in the establishment and development of the Company of the East Indies (VOC) created in the United Provinces of Holland, 1725.

Bottom: French map of the trading post of Tranquebar, mid-17th century.

Times of Glory and Profit

'We predominantly focused on commerce which entails long voyages, having been persuaded by common sense and by the experience of our neighbours that profit outweighs, by far, the toil and trouble of invading distant countries,' declared Louis XIV, in August 1664.

French settlements in India followed one after another: Pondicherry in 1674, Chandernagor in 1688. Then, after a long pause, Mahe in 1721 and Yanam in 1731; Karaikal became a permanent part of the territory in 1738. These new settlements ushered in a prosperous period for the French, thanks to the activity of the Compagnie des Indes Orientales.

Opposite page: The Regent, Philippe d'Orléans, as protector of Indian trade with the Indies, Antoine Dieu, Château de Versailles. Pic.© RMN.

Top: 'I will flourish wherever I go': detail of the arms of the Compagnie des Indes Orientales. Musée de la Compagnie des Indes, Lorient.

Compagnie des Indes Orientales

'By the grace of God, Louis, King of France and Navarre, greets all present here and those to come! By our Declaration of 1664, we founded a powerful company of our subjects from all walks of life to trade with the Indies.' It is with these words that the royal declaration of 1666 opens, making Lorient the main centre of the Compagnie des Indes Orientales. The idea of a merchant company under the patronage of the state was to last for over a century. However, following the Franco-British War of 1688-1693, which paralysed the shipping companies, the Compagnie des Indes Orientales soon slipped into bankruptcy. The ship owners of Saint-Malo could not save it.

In 1719, during the Regency of Philippe d'Orléans, and on the initiative of John Law, a new company was created – the Compagnie Perpétuelle des Indes. Like its predecessor, it was a company of privileges. The king guaranteed the exclusive right to trade expecting this would re-establish the kingdom's finances and wipe out its debts. The merchants, following the example of their English and Dutch counterparts, formed a Board of Directors, incorporating the king ex officio, and pooled their capital to finance trading voyages. Board privileges included control of all goods from abroad, the right to dispense justice in the name of the king and even to maintain and use an army in the name of king and country. Unlike its predecessor, the new company handled all goods, from both the East and the West Indies. Private individuals, and particularly agents of the Company, were authorised by the king to exploit existing commercial routes for their own profit; that is, to follow the already existing trade routes to India from Japan and down to

Top: Baluster vase, porcelain, glazed polychrome enamel, China – reign of Kangxi (1662-1722), about 1710.
Opposite page: A view of the port of Lorient in 1776 by Louis-François Cassas (1756-1827). Musée de la Compagnie des Indes, Lorient.

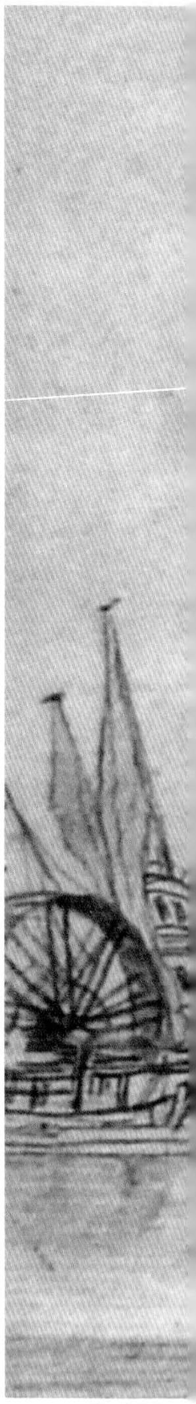

Africa. Finally, to attract more investors, the king announced that noblemen were allowed to trade without risk of losing their rank, ensuring that both gentry as well as aristocrats no longer disregarded the opportunity for wealth and riches opening up to them.

The Company set up its office in Paris in the Hotel Tubœuf, close by the Stock Exchange and the Royal Library. But its real headquarters were located at Port Louis in Brittany, thanks to the king's donation of this property. This is the place that became Lorient. It was a new town built entirely by the Company, owing everything, including its name, to its trading activities. In 1752, Mignot de Montigny observed on visiting Brittany: 'This burgeoning town is quite pretty, well situated and neatly constructed; it seems destined to gain in importance.' In less than fifty years, the little town of a few thousand inhabitants would become a real city with a population of 50,000. Like Brest, the rare deep-water port was strategically located and protected from enemy attacks by a fortress. As Montigny explained: 'At Lorient the Compagnie des Indes Orientales [commonly known as Compagnie Perpétuelle des Indes] has gathered together its naval, military and commercial interests to create one of the finest naval yards of the kingdom.' It had set up there its dockyards, barracks for training Company troops and one part of its administrative premises, together with a sales house.

Above: 'Weavers', lithograph, early 19th century.

At Lorient, the Company was looking to develop lucrative business opportunities. On its route to the West Indies, it experimented with triangular trade in Africa. It traded in slaves and manufactured goods, as it did with the sugar and cotton trade in Louisiana, and to the north with the fur trade in Quebec. In the East Indies, the attractions were fine textiles, notably silks, and printed textile, plants for dyeing, and spices, among which pepper was the most sought after. According to the local lore of the time: 'Pepper is hot and makes

Goods and trade in 18th-century India

Pondicherry served as a warehouse for local goods and those in transit, coming from the East Indies and China. When a trading voyage was scheduled, Indian merchants were charged with preparing the cargo, paying the producers in advance. Six months later, the Company would buy the goods from the merchants and store them in the citadel, awaiting shipping. Most of the commodities shown below were bought in modern times in Pondicherry's Grand Bazaar, closely resembling the products traded in the Indian Ocean and the China Sea in the eighteenth century.

Routes and trading posts beyond Cape Town

The territory of the Compagnie des Indes Orientales extended over four continents. To reap the expected profits, it had to establish a permanent presence in this vast area.

Below: Appendix of M. Dupleix's *Memoir*, comparing the value of goods despatched to India and that of exports to Europe during his governorship.

Right: Map of sea routes to India from Cape Town. Appendix to M. Le Gentil's *Travels*. Note the long and the short routes from the Mascareigne Islands.

Below: Frontispiece of Luillier's *Nouveau Voyage aux Grandes Indes*, 1726.

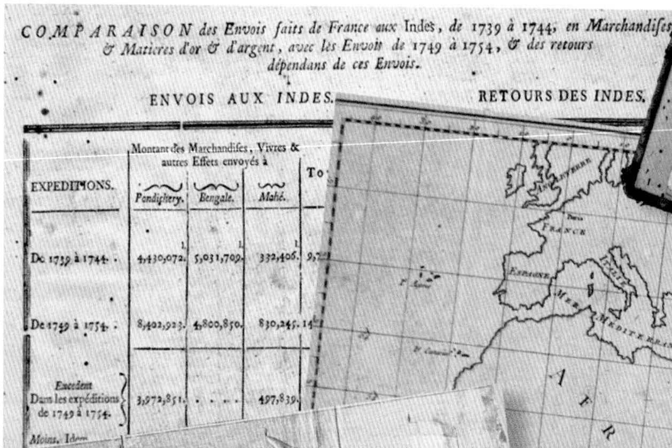
COMPARAISON des Envois faits de France aux Indes, de 1739 à 1744, en Marchandises & Matieres d'or & d'argent, avec les Envois de 1749 à 1754, & des retours dépendans de ces Envois.

ENVOIS AUX INDES. RETOURS DES INDES.

EXPEDITIONS.	Montant des Marchandises, Vivres & autres Effets envoyés à Pondichery.	Bengale.	Mahé.	To
De 1739 à 1744.	l. 4,430,072.	l. 5,031,709.	l. 332,406.	9,7
De 1749 à 1754.	8,402,923.	4,800,850.	830,245.	14
Excedent Dans les expéditions de 1749 à 1754.	3,972,851.	. . . .	497,839.	
Moins. Idem				

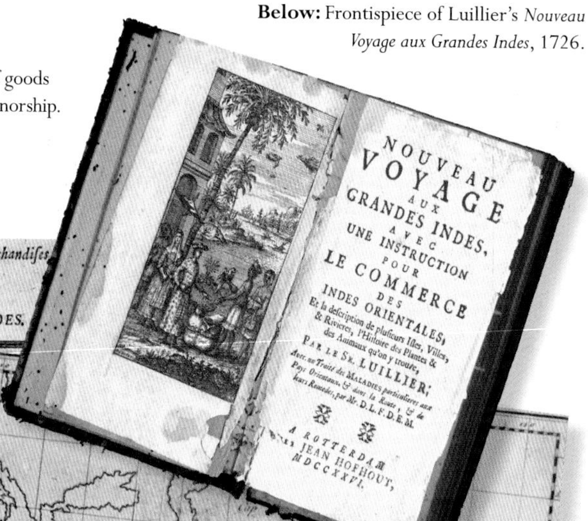
NOUVEAU VOYAGE AUX GRANDES INDES, AVEC UNE INSTRUCTION POUR LE COMMERCE DES INDES ORIENTALES, Et la description de plusieurs Isles, Villes, & Rivieres, l'Histoire des Plantes & des Animaux qu'on y trouve, PAR LE SR. LUILLIER; Avec un Traité des MALADIES particulieres aux Pays Orientaux, & dans la Route, & de leurs Remedes, par Mr. D. L. F. D. E. M.

A ROTTERDAM, Chez JEAN HOFHOUT, MDCCXXVI.

Above: View of the European quarter of Canton in the 18th century.

Right: Golden pagodas and a copper *doudou*. From 1736 onwards, the French colonial administration was authorised to mint its own currency. The coin in the left is a *doudou* (copper coin for everyday transactions) from Pondicherry, mid-18th century.

you urinate, it helps the digestion, improves the eyesight and is effective against wild animal bites.' In the far East at Canton, the products which were the most in demand were tea and Chinese curios – precious utensils, embroidered silk and ornate furniture were brought to Pondicherry to be dispatched. The Jetsam was ordinarily constituted of a cargo of saltpetre, redwoods and, from further north, in Bengal, small shells called cowries, which were used in Africa as currency, especially to buy slaves. There was also small scale trading of opium, essentially for medicinal purposes. In return, the company's vessels brought all the basic supplies needed to sustain European trading posts: arms, alcohol, all kinds of drapes, and, as a consideration towards Indian magnates, some high quality artistic items. But the most precious cargo consisted of solid gold and silver pieces, some of these from the South American mines, which were used for company purchases. An anonymous satirist writing in 1719 concluded: 'Europe would have been infinitely richer, had it never known this country.'

Long-distance trade on such a global scale required extraordinary funding. Among the heaviest investments, in addition to those related to the sizable fleet, anywhere between twenty to seventy vessels were those needed to set up resting points. These served two functions: first, as warehouses, and second, as ports of call for supplies and the repair and maintenance of ships. The journey from France to Pondicherry and back took from twelve to eighteen months – and from China almost two years. Consequently, the Company established settlements in Gorée and Saint Louis in Senegal, and in Saint Domingue

Above: *Le Massiac*, a 900-ton ship. 1:24 scale model by Jean Delouche. Like all Compagnie des Indes ships, it had a wide-mouthed body suitable for the transport of merchandise. Musée de la Compagnie des Indes, Lorient.

in the West Indies. In the Indian Ocean the Company selected the 'Île de Bourbon', 'Île de France', and also Moka on the Arabian Coast to better supply the major trading post at Pondicherry or the Chinese town of Canton.

However, profits were slow to come in. Initial investment was very high, and cash flows took decades to trickle through.

Above: Brahma and his consort Saraswati, plate from Pierre Sonnerat's travels, end 18th century.

The Compagnie was in direct competition with the British East India Company and the Dutch Vereenigde Ooste Indische Company, and had to carve a place for itself in the Indian market, which meant additional investment. The difficulties increased because of the failure to modernise banking practices and the creation of a bond-issuing bank. It was an example of state capitalism before its time. The failure of John Law's Bank, which worked hand in hand with the Compagnie des Indes Orientales, had unprecedented consequences in March 1720. Then there was the mercantilist mindset of the royal administration in France to take into consideration, which strove to promote the re-exportation of goods from France to the rest of Europe, and to protect the French textile industry. Under pressure from the Lyon manufacturers, imports of silks and *Indiennes*, coloured cotton fabric, were banned. Moreover, the improvement in supply provided by these trading posts, pushed prices on the French market down and profits gradually diminished during the eighteenth century. Nevertheless, by the end of the 1730s, the major obstacles had been removed, and the Company started earning profits comparable to those of the British East India Company.

Right: 'Sinus Gangeticus Vulgo Golfo De Bengala', Dutch map by Jan Jansson, Amsterdam, 1650.

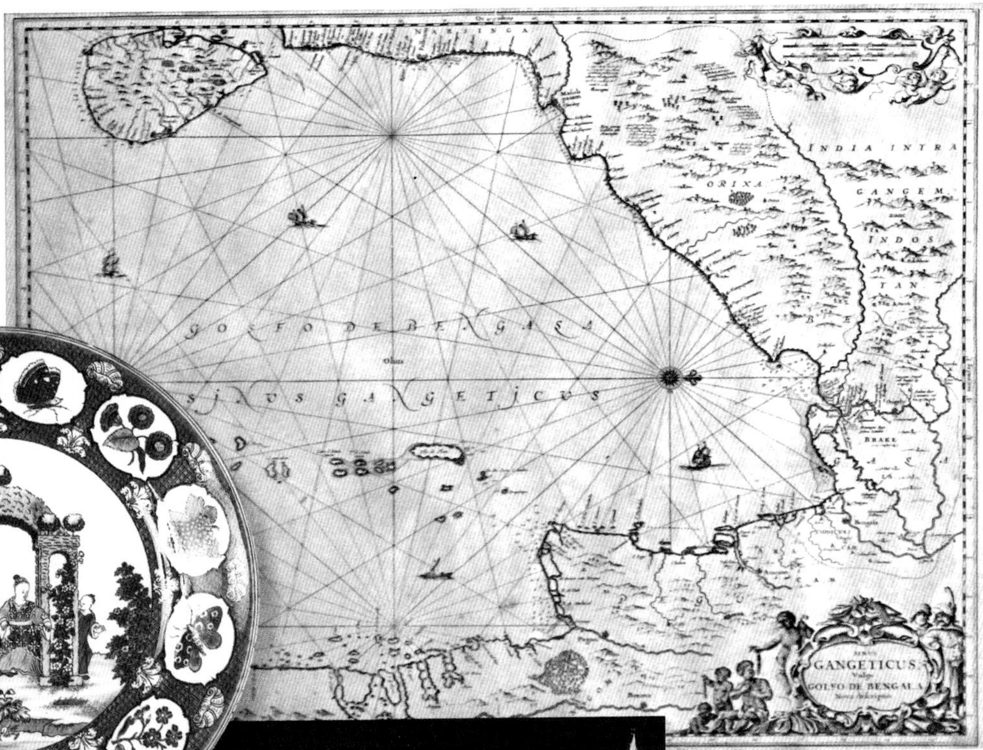

Below: Arbour decoration, blue glaze and gold porcelain plate, China – reign of Qianlong (1736-1795), about 1737. Musée de la Compagnie des Indes, Lorient.

Left: Section view of *Le Massiac*, a ship belonging to the Compagnie des Indes, on her return from India. Redrawn at 1:42 scale by Jean Delouche, 1976.

A Dot on the Indian Map

'It is ten o'clock in the morning and I'm writing to say that after, that is to say, we have anchored in front of Pondicherry. The place looks beautiful, but I don't see a fort anywhere. I am told, however, that there is one.' This observation made on 12 August 1690 by a writer employed in the Royal Navy, one Robert Challes, is most revealing of the times. In the early days the situation of French trading posts was a delicate matter – set up through agreement or by gift, the right to settle permanently was granted to or withheld from Europeans by South Indian princes. And so it was that access to Pondicherry was granted in December 1672, by the local ruler of the region, Sher Khan Lodi of Valkondapuram representing the Bijapur kingdom. Benoît Bellanger de Lespinay took up residence in 1673. In February 1673, the latter took possession of the place in the name of the French king and of the Compagnie with François Martin, his main employee, in charge. In this way, the wily Sher Khan expected the French to set up in competition against the Dutch, already well established at Porto Novo and in Goudelour and also requiring an occasional military help.

However, the relative ease with which authorisations for these settlements could be obtained belied the fact that they could also be just as easily revoked when wars or

Below: Pondicherry attacked by the Dutch in 1693. From the original drawning of a Jesuit father. The Dutch fleet is facing the 'Barlong' fort, and artillery has just been unloaded.

Opposite page: French map of the Indian peninsula in the second quarter of the 18th century, modern colouring.

GOLCONDA
DECAN
VISAPOUR
BISNAGAR vel CARNATE
GINGI
MAISOUR
MADURE
TANSCHAUR
MARAVA
CANARA
Terra Chira naiken
COTE DE MALABAR
COTE DE COROMANDEL
PARTIE DU GOLFE DE BENGALA
COTE DE LA PECHERIE
DETROIT CHILAO
INS. CEYLON
Rm CICOCOL vel CIACOLA
Golconda
Masulipatan A.G.H.
Madraspatan l. Fort S. George A.
S. Thome l. Meliapour
Sandras patnam H.
Pondichery G.
Fort S. David
Porta Nova H.
Tranquebar D.
Negapadnam H.
Visagapatan
Narsinga l. Narsingapatan
Nelour H.
Tripiti l. Tripante
Pandale
Ghandeyry l.
Bisnagar
Kaman
Trichenapali
Madure
Trimularachiam
Almada
Raolconda
Ponda P.
H. Coutchien l.
Cochin
A.C.H. Calicut
H. Rm Cranganoor
Rm Porrat H.
H. Travancor
Cap Comorin
Nota
Jafanapatan
Candy
Cotta
Trinquimale H.
Batecalo H.
H. Colombo
Explicatio Signorum
A. Angli
D. Dani
G. Galli
H. Hollandi
P. Portugalli
Milliaria Gallica marina
Milliaria Germanica
Milliaria Indica
Mill. Malabarica & Coromand.
MALABAR & COROMANDEL
CEYLON

Above:
Detail of black and white lithograph, elephant set for parade, early 19th century.

Below:
Coloured lithograph, Raja or Hindu prince, early 19th century.

revolutions broke out. Sher Khan Lodi's star quickly faded in the face of the rising power of the Maratha king Shivaji whilst already in 1693 the new ruler of Gingee Fort who controlled the whole Tamil region, Raja Ram, sold the emerging city of Pondicherry (under the feet of the French) to the Dutch. Following a declaration of war between France and the Netherlands, the place was immediately besieged and retaken. In 1699, Pondicherry was returned to the French in exchange for reparations according to the terms of the Ryswick peace treaty

The unstable political situation in South India meant that the settlements were inevitably fragile. Robert Challes wrote already in 1690: 'Earlier, this region belonged to the Mughals and later, one of its generals, named Sombagi or Shevahi, usurped it. His son is presently the ruler but because of his immaturity, his authority is weak.' Time would resolve the problem, much to the perplexity of the French. The Marathas from the Northwest made several raids on the Deccan plateau, maintaining a strong pressure on the southern kingdoms. At the same time, the Mughals sought to reassert their sovereignty over the southern kingdoms, whose autonomy had become an irritant. Consequently, as in the past, the kings had a certain self-interest in allying with the Europeans, often playing them off, one against the other, and using them against the Marathas or the Mughals. Meanwhile, the local aristocracy continued to fill their coffers, whilst the splendour of their courts, even under suzerainty, reached previously unknown levels of magnificence, due to inflows of gold and, especially, silver from international commerce. As for royal power in the region, it was reinforced by the fact that palace coffers were full enough to maintain large private armies. All this wealth naturally provoked jealousies and conflicts of interests which only served to further destabilise the region. As a result of this uncertainty an intricate network of dangerous alliances developed around the European settlements, which themselves

Above: Hasan, Persian noblewoman. ©EFEO

became drawn into local Indian politics. By 1730, the French had fully grasped the Indian context. As Charpentier de Cossigny, an engineer of the Company, wrote: 'Not a week goes by here when the Governor does not receive a delegation of Moorish princes or Gentiles or a visit from one of those regional country lords, always with the greatest of pomp possible, to promote a favourable image of the nation.'

From its early days on, Pondicherry remained an active centre for textile production; however, there was no town planning to speak of. There would only have been several vast gardens and a village of a few mud-and-brick houses clustered around ancient temples, all that remained of the former Olukarai. When François Martin first arrived, the place appeared to be occupied by small villages with Macouas of the fishing caste, living in the midst of coconut plantations and paddy fields... During the first decade, the French settlement was limited to a few European buildings used as warehouses to the east of present day Pondicherry, whilst the construction of a chapel soon followed. It wasn't long before the efforts of François Martin bore fruit and a number of weavers came to settle nearby.

In a nutshell, the French trading posts were far from being operational and the ever practical Challes asked himself in his journal 'why the Company hadn't yet got around to constructing a wharf'. There was no port worthy of the name in any of the five French trading posts, even though Pondicherry offered one of the best anchorages on the Coromandel coast. Challes explained: 'Neither launches nor dinghies are able to approach the shore at more than gunshot's distance, because the breakers are so powerful that to approach any closer would be to invite death.' Passengers and goods had to be disembarked on flat-bottomed rowboats, called *chelingues* rowed by the Macouas. If a hurricane broke out, ships would go further out to sea, because proximity to the sandbar at such time would mean certain disaster.

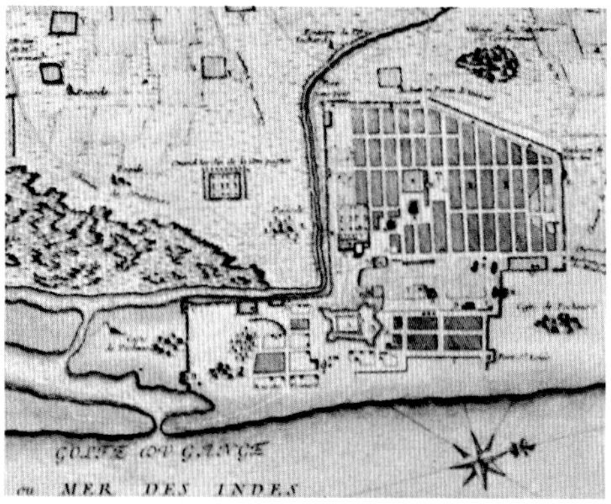

Above: Plan of Pondicherry in 1705 by Nicolas de Fer.
Opposite page: 'Plan of Pondicherry town and citadel (Fort Louis)', anonymous, 1739. CAOM, Aix-en-Provence, DFC 32b 20bis. © CAOM.

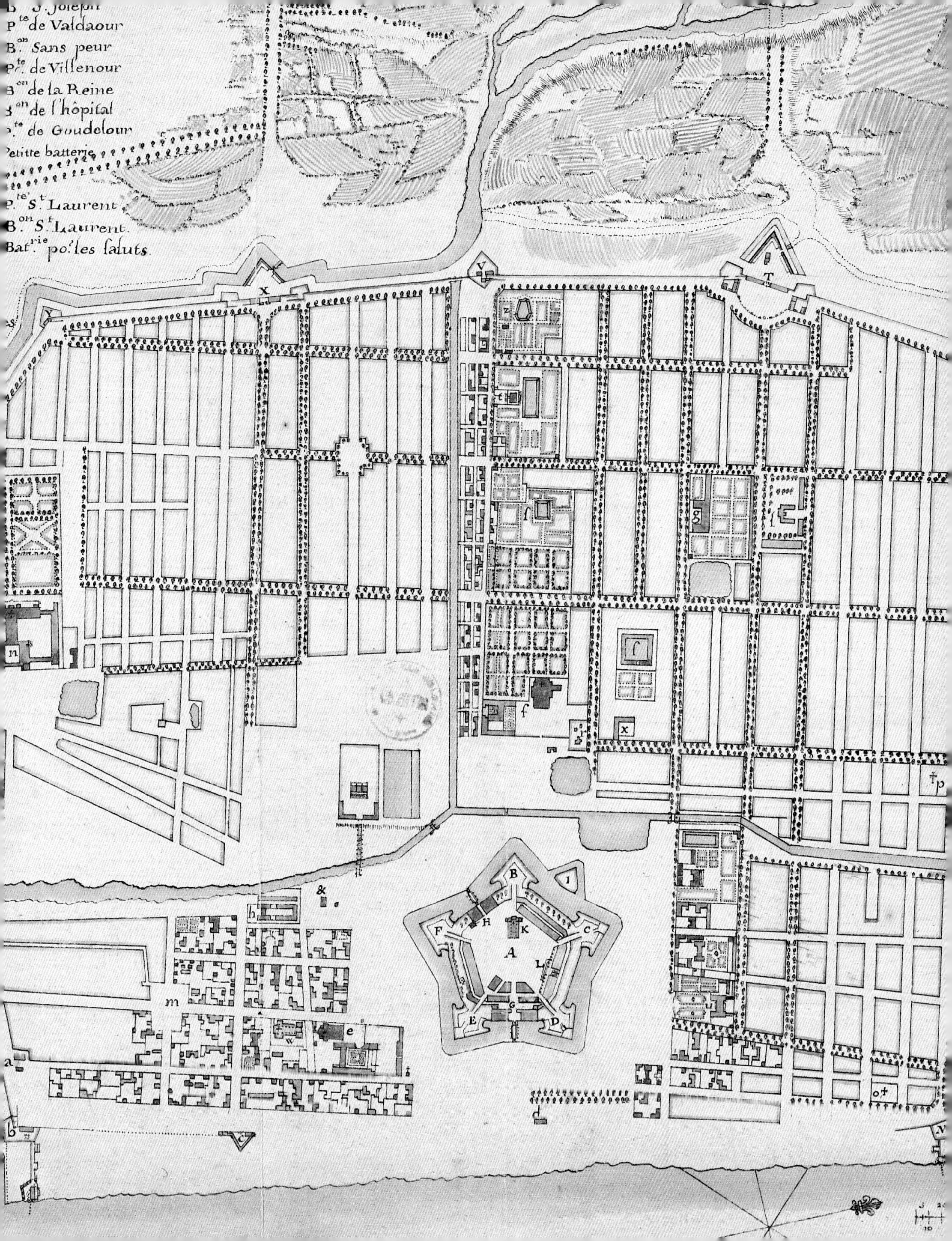

S.t Joseph
P.te de Valdaour
B.on Sans peur
P.te de Villenour
B.on de la Reine
B.on de l'hôpital
P.te de Goudelour
Petitte batterie
P.te S.t Laurent
B.on S.t Laurent
Bat.rie po.r les saluts

Fort Louis at the times of Dupleix's glory

Fort Louis of Pondicherry was the undisputable symbol of French power in India in the 18th century. The construction was entrusted to the engineer Denis de Nyon and was executed from 1702 onwards.
Inspired by the famous works of Louis XIV's chief engineer, Maréchal Vauban, the fortress in Pondicherry was a miniature copy of the one in Tournais.

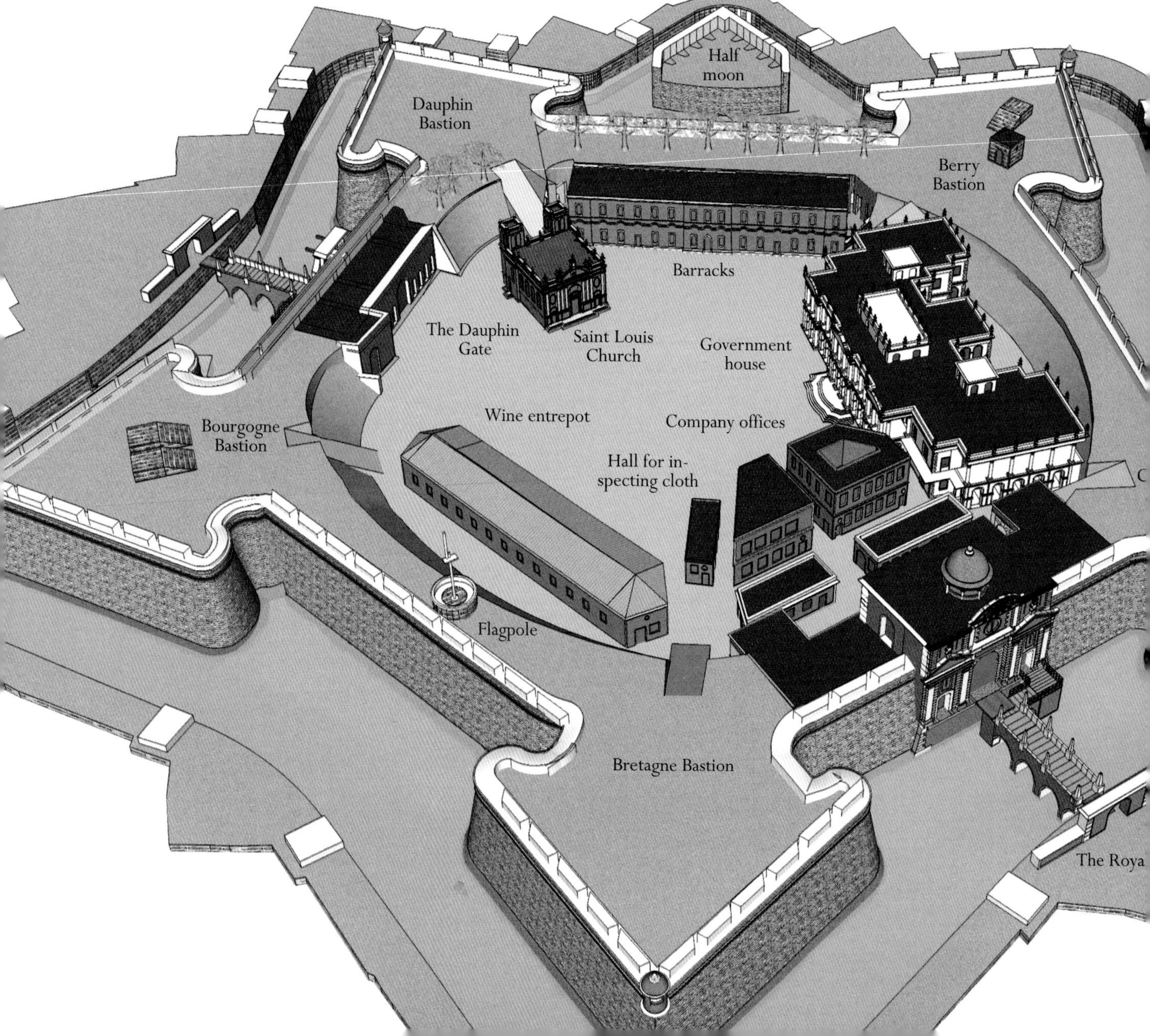

A Burgeoning City

The first assignment of the governors sent to India by the Company was to consolidate the settlements. As early as 1688, François Martin succeeded in gaining permission from the Nawab of Gingee to build fortifications. He started with construction of the first boundary protection, 'the palm barrier', which enclosed the town. A fort soon followed. Challes described it as 'barlong', 'very irregular, with three shabby round towers, and protected only on the park side, where there is a normal bastion.' But the spacious urban design, which is still characteristic of Pondicherry, was laid out during the Dutch occupation between 1693 and 1699. With the return of the French in 1699, François Martin and his successors gradually implemented the original Dutch checker board plan. A 1705 map drawn up by the royal French cartographer, Nicolas de Fer, indicates the emergence of two distinct centres, one near the small European fort and the other towards the west, at the intersection of the Villianur road. The southern limits of the town were marked by the Oupar river. The European and the Indian quarters were separated by a depressed and insalubrious area, but the later 'symbolic' canal boundary between the 'white' and the 'black' township was not yet apparent.

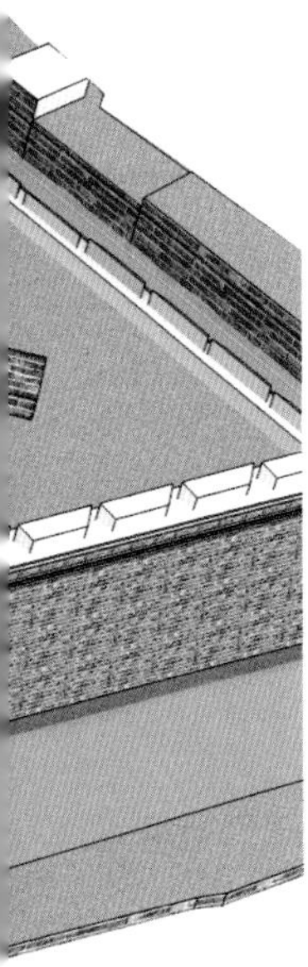

From 1700 onwards, the obvious defensive weakness of these fortifications forced the Compagnie des Indes Orientales to invest in a fort capable of protecting Pondicherry from nautical attack. Between 1702 and 1706, on the southern part of what is today Barathi Square, a major Maréchal Vauban style star fortress, le Fort Louis, was constructed. This obvious sign of power and stability was also meant to attract the Indian populations which swelled rapidly in Pondicherry. In 1710 the inhabitants numbered more than 60,000. It was therefore necessary to create a new quarter for them in the city. Between 1721 and 1735, under Governor Lenoir, an elliptical wall was erected to allow the optimal use of artillery. Governor Joseph François Dupleix completed the seaward fortifications with the construction of the Marine Gate. He then completed work on the palatial new Government Headquarters begun under Governor Dumas, 'One could call the Government seat the Palace of the Indies, as it is not possible to imagine anything so beautiful and ornate in that country; it astonishes all those who see it. Everything is extremely refined and reflects an infinite taste, embellished with bas-reliefs and well-executed figures,' reported a visiting naval captain. In 1742, the simple comparison of the layout of Pondicherry and that of Madras reveals how far the Company's challenge to make Pondicherry a capital of South India had succeeded.

The high scale of investment in Pondicherry was driven by the Compagnie des Indes Orientales back in France. As the most profitable trading post, Pondicherry was to be the centre of commercial operations in India and should provide protection for goods from other trading posts or *loges*. The governor appointed to Pondicherry presided over the Supreme Council of the Colony that was responsible for dispensing justice and implementing decisions. Directors of all the other trading posts would be convened by the governor who in turn presided over local council meetings comprised of different key local functionaries. In 1725 Dupleix filled one of these posts, as Commissioner of Company troops. The importance played by hierarchy in Pondicherry, as in the other trading posts, was reinforced by the presence of direct Company representatives. An interesting example would be that of the Company Prosecutor, responsible for overseeing business transactions. At that time a garrison of several hundred marines of the Company was permanently on duty, although the number of sepoys (Indian soldiers) was already much larger. However, everyone was well aware that India was unstable and changing, while France and the Company were far away.

Opposite: View of Pondicherry, circa 1750, anonymous, oil on canvas (20th century). Painted from a document of the period, it is one of the rare realistic views of Pondicherry in the 18th century.

A Strange Confrontation

The trading posts gave rise to their own very peculiar social development. From the outset, Pondicherry society was basically composed of Indians interested in doing business with Europeans. The rapid settlement of the 'new town', for European travellers the 'town of love affairs', shows the ease with which Indians adapted to a European style of urban living. Most probably the European chess grid was fully adapted to the particularities of Indian society.

The centre for all important dealings was the Big Bazaar. Beyond the smooth running of commerce, the French were very eager to use this natural forum to settle local issues, such as legal and caste affairs. The organisation of Indian temple communities corresponded to that of the streets: Rue des Cométis was the street of the Chettys, or merchants, Rue des Choulias, grouped the mattress-makers. But there were also streets of the tile-makers, the Brahmins, streets of courtesans (insultingly nicknamed 'Whore Street' by the Dutch). Two more communities were part of this coherent society. The Muslims, called 'Moors' by the Europeans, though present in the old town from the outset, were soon moved to the south, into the new districts of the 'black' town. Their wealth, power and usefulness to the French were such that this area was not subjected to the constraints of the master-plan. And finally, there were the Pariahs and the very low castes, who lived on the outskirts of town in two designated areas and who were equally marginalised in social terms, being, responsible for all menial jobs, including serving the Europeans. In fact, from a European perspective, the Indian system of castes set within a rationally-planned town seems to have created a perfect pre-industrial organisation wholly given over to production and the maintenance of a large city.

On the 'white' town side, Europeans, still few in number, constructed well-ventilated big houses for themselves facing the wind coming from the sea. It's a vital matter of hygiene. 'The Company people

Left: 'Worldly' Brahmin or interpreters, lithograph, early 19th century.

Rank and Wealth in 18th-century Pondicherry

10. Terrace, with a staircase leading to it, a place for relaxation.

9. Inner courtyard and outhouses.

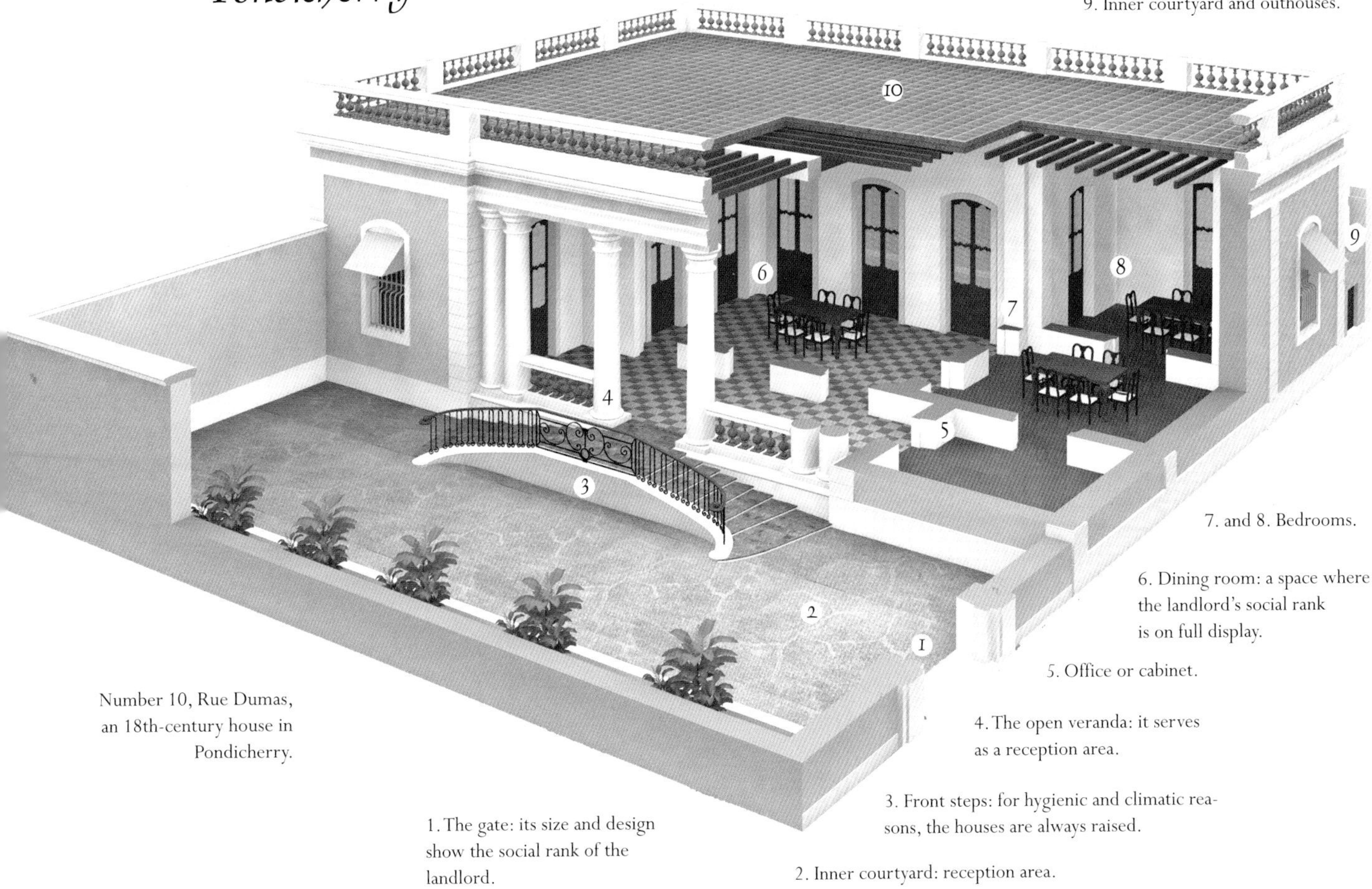

7. and 8. Bedrooms.

6. Dining room: a space where the landlord's social rank is on full display.

5. Office or cabinet.

4. The open veranda: it serves as a reception area.

3. Front steps: for hygienic and climatic reasons, the houses are always raised.

2. Inner courtyard: reception area.

1. The gate: its size and design show the social rank of the landlord.

Number 10, Rue Dumas, an 18th-century house in Pondicherry.

are not difficult to make out,' observes Robert Challes. 'They are so pale, livid, thin and hideous, that if I had not seen them carrying a sword, I would have mistaken them for a reincarnation of Lazarus or at least for the monks of Notre-Dame de la Trappe. They are so lacking in strength, that one gust of wind would fell them.' Under the burning climate of Pondicherry, mortality among the Europeans was high, and one out of two employees sent to Asia died of fevers. But in Pondicherry, they had the opportunity to get rich. Working as merchants or as soldiers, they had ample time to conduct their own businesses. Even though the Company's wages were quite inadequate, there was ample opportunity for resourceful people to succeed.

Although Company employees constituted the core of the 'white' town, they were not the only Europeans. In fact right from the outset, the Topas of Indo-Portuguese origin or 'hat-donning' creoles, settled in the 'white' town. Clearly of mixed race, they were Christian and as such they were firmly connected to the white society through intermarriage. Lastly, in the course of the eighteenth century, the success of the Company and the dreams of new fortunes that it fuelled, ensured a weak but constant flow of immigrants to Pondicherry, to the extent that it gave rise to a European middle class, made up mainly of craftsmen, and discharged soldiers and mercenaries of various nationalities, all determined to climb the rungs of social hierarchy.

But most of the time and through tacit understanding, these different members of society did not seek any other contact except within the context of work. As Christians and Catholics, the Europeans considered themselves superior to the rest of society; people of mixed race (*métis*) ranked themselves above the Hindus, while the Hindus considered the other two categories as impure, the mere contact with whom required frequent purificatory ablutions.

In these conditions, there was no other way to put together Company ship cargoes, than to appeal to Indian middlemen who moved between the frontiers of language and prejudice with considerable skill. They were called the *dubash*. Most of the Europeans had one or even two at their service. But the Company selected their *dubash* from the most rich and influential families, to ensure they could navigate local political and economic entanglements. By 1742, Ananda Ranga Pillai was advancing money to the Company, organising production, and representing the Indian population before the governor. Between the *dubash* and his employer a relationship of trust was essential.

Ananda Ranga Pillai

Right:

Ananda Ranga Pillai's portrait at the age of thirty-five. He was the most famous Indian broker of the Compagnie des Indes Orientales. Commerce demanded that the Europeans communicated in the local languages. In each trading post, the job of interpreter was entrusted to the *dubash*, 'one who speaks two languages', who more often than not was a Christian, and the *dubash* soon became a necessary and recognised intermediary.

The profession passed on from father to son, thus Ananda Ranga Pillai inherited the job from his father, Tiruvengadam I. However, as a Hindu, he owed his nomination entirely to the favour of Governor Dupleix, who was struck by his extraordinary business flair.

From being an interpreter, he soon became a broker, and then the *dewan*, or the governor's counsellor. He wrote his diary from 1736 to 1761, one of the rare primary secular texts in Tamil. It is a meticulous, personal, day-to-day account of the crucial years of the French in India.

Left: Ananda Ranga Pillai's house, constructed in 1738, shows the blend of styles in the residences of rich brokers. Although the ground floor is in the traditional style, the upper floor follows the European canons of the period. (© Sebastian Cortes)

'New Rome of the Indies'

The Catholic Church played a critical role in such a small trading-post society. In 1726, while calling at port, Chevalier d'Albert noted: 'There are three churches in Pondicherry; the first is at the fort serving the garrison and Company employees, the second is in the town, a Capuchin church for Europeans – the Reverend Capuchin Fathers conduct service in both these churches – and the third is run by the Reverend Jesuit Fathers for those dressed in Indian clothes. This form of distinguishing between parishes provokes division and jealousy amongst them.'

The merchant companies, as servants of their respective monarchs, themselves God's lieutenants on earth, were duty-bound to facilitate the promotion of Christianity and the arrival of missionaries. Although the Portuguese had already created several Catholic missions, particularly in the region of Goa and Madurai, after their decline France was the only effective power to promote and protect Catholicism in India. Pondicherry, recognised rather late as a dioceses was one such centre. Many Catholic congregations established their bases here and in due course spread across South India as well as across the whole of South-Asia.

Missionary activities started as soon as the settlement was set up. In 1674,

Background: Lithography by Cabassol, 'View of the Jesuits church'. Circa 1839.

François Martin invited a few Capuchin Fathers already established in Madras to come to Pondicherry. Father Cosme served as the first chaplain of the French. Though they provided for the religious needs of the Europeans and Creoles, they also began to convert the high castes. Thus, in 1684, the *dubash* Lazare de Mota gave them a plot located near the fort which was later shifted by the Company to land in the south part of the city. On this very spot, they built the first Our Lady of the Angels Church in 1707. The political situation in Siam brought back the other congregation mentioned by d'Albert. The Society of Jesus was indeed the greatest: Father Tachard's Jesuits came to Pondicherry in 1689 and they embarked upon educational and evangelical work with Indians of all castes and with people of mixed race who were rejected by both communities. They received permission from the Archbishop of San Thome to form a new mission and received the letters patent from the French King in 1695. The first church was erected in the midst of the 'black' town. Razed by the Dutch in 1693, it was soon restored in 1699. Jesuits have made their mark in India, including one of the founding members, François Xavier, who became the second Catholic saint of India (after Saint Thomas). The Jesuits were followed by the missionaries of the Society of the Foreign Missions of Paris who failed to establish a real foothold until 1771 when they decided to create an important seminary in Veerampattinam where indigenous priests from all over Asia would be instructed. In 1777, a strong French wind of anticlericalism overthrew the Jesuits who were eventually forced to merge into the Society of the Foreign Mission of Paris. Often profoundly intellectual and disciplined instruments of their order, missionaries ventured to the remotest areas, patiently studying the language and customs there, writing numerous reports, books and dictionaries in order to create the tools of evangelism – tools which were also those of colonisation – and building churches, monasteries, convents, cathedrals and seminaries.

Left: Penitent from Malabar, coloured lithograph, 18th century.

But finding new converts in India proved a less than simple task. Hindus remained tolerant of anything new, as long as it did not disturb their traditions. Missionary work was not as effective as in America. Polytheism, viewed as nonsensical by missionaries, continued unabated. However, the missionaries did attain a certain hold in remote mountain areas and in urban societies in contact with European customs, where, in order to get people to follow them, they had to modify certain Christian rites by including some Hindu practices. *Les Lettres Édifiantes et Curieuses Écrites des Missions Étrangères*, published at the end of the eighteenth century, described the missionaries well: 'After having learnt the language and customs of the country, the missionaries dress like Indian penitents' and 'adopt all their customs and practices, sitting cross-legged on the floor, and eating there too, without touching anything with the left hand, which, according to these people, would go completely against the rules of politeness and propriety.' Beside this, missionaries also allowed processions to imitate Hindu rituals and the dates of certain Christian festivals were fixed in accordance with the Hindu calendar. Marriages between blood-relations were

Below: Watercolour, early 19th century. Christ at rest in his tomb and the adoration of the Virgin Mary. The scene is set in Pondicherry.

given dispensations by the Pope himself and the customs of various castes were permitted even inside the church precinct. This tendency ultimately triggered a serious religious debate, the question of the Malabar rituals, to which Chevalier d'Albert alluded and which shook the whole of Christendom, far beyond the confines of Pondicherry.

The question of Malabar rituals was a divisive issue among missionaries in Pondicherry, as well as in other places. The Capuchin Fathers were quite tolerant, but curiously the Jesuits showed much more reserve. They asked the Supreme Council of Pondicherry to wall up the temple gates within the town, to forbid Hindu processions on Sundays and to preserve the right to hold honorary functions for Christians alone.

French governors were also unsure about the approach to follow. They felt morally bound to support the Catholic Church, but they knew they were also duty bound to protect and promote the activities of the Company in Pondicherry. Any religious zeal was a threat which could jeopardise trade: in 1715 the ban on Hindu processions on Sundays resulted in an exodus of weavers and the Supreme Council had to reverse the ban in order to preserve the commercial activity of the town. In 1733, the Company pushed through regulations, which mentioned that 'all ceremonies which constitute the essence of their religion should be wisely tolerated.' But a few governors such as Dupleix were more than willing to use their authority to further the Jesuit cause. He forced Indian slaves to adopt Christianity, forbade all work on Sundays and gave the missionaries the incomes of two villages. When the Jesuits complained loudly about a temple dedicated to Iswaran, which adjoined their church, Dupleix finally followed their wishes and in 1748 sanctioned the demolition with little or no resistance from the town.

Below: Watercolour, early 19th century from Our Lady of the Sacred Heart Church in Pondicherry.

In 1703, the missionaries reported a population of 2,000 converts in Pondicherry with great satisfaction. But how many starving peasants would have renounced their new religion at the first sight of a lull after a calamity? How many converted notables such as Guarappa, son of the *dubash* Nyappa, would have secretly continued to adore the gods of their ancestors? All these endeavours notwithstanding, the end result on the eve of the nineteenth century was rather lacklustre. The Catholic Church could lay claim to only 10 or 15 per cent of the town's population and in the countryside the percentage of the converts may well have been below 2 per cent.

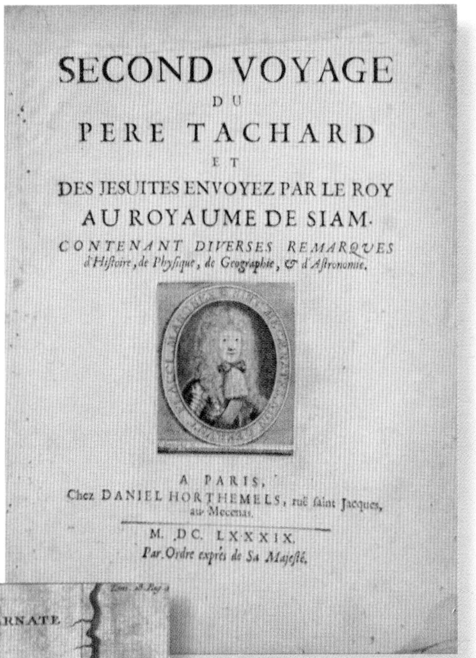
SECOND VOYAGE
DU
PERE TACHARD
ET
DES JESUITES ENVOYEZ PAR LE ROY
AU ROYAUME DE SIAM.
CONTENANT DIVERSES REMARQUES
d'Histoire, de Physique, de Geographie, & d'Astronomie.

A PARIS,
Chez DANIEL HORTHEMELS, ruë saint Jacques, au Mecenas.
M. DC. LXXXIX.
Par Ordre exprès de Sa Majesté.

Above: Account of Father Tachard, founder of the Pondicherry Mission and evangelist of Siam, 1689.

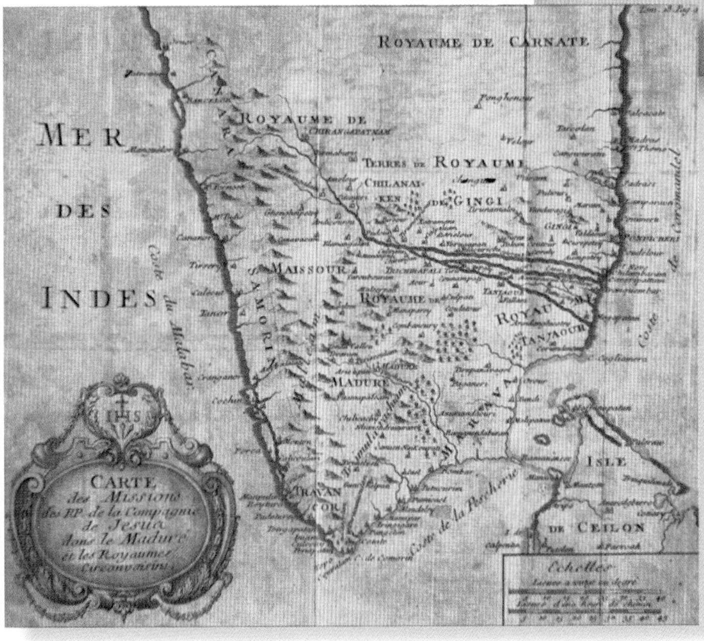

Left: Map of the Reverend Fathers' Missions of the Society of Jesus in Madurai and the neighbouring kingdoms, circa 1750. The Jesuits were present in the coastal ports, in the capitals, and along the Cauvery and its delta.

French India and British India

It is often said that the first half of the eighteenth century constituted a golden age for the French in India. Yet the question still remains whether this positive view of the adventures of Dupleix and the French in India, is the result of history being misunderstood across the vagaries of time and distance. His genius was perhaps not that of a great military figure, but surely it lay in his being able to understand that India could herself be the source of finance for commercial ventures. In less eulogous form, Ananda Ranga Pillai wrote: 'Monsieur Lenoir worked like a gardener. He enriched the earth, ploughed, fertilised and prepared his crops. He planted trees which blossomed and whose fruit he enjoyed during his time. Monsieur Dumas simply devoured the produce. In Monsieur Dupleix's time, a tempest devoured the garden.'

Dupleix was the fifth governor of Pondicherry. His father was a royal civil servant and stakeholder in the Compagnie des Indes who collected honorary titles by acquiring various offices. Joseph François Dupleix, born in 1697, was considered unstable by his disapproving father who sought to channel his conduct by arranging his exile. Using his influence, the father bought his son the title of First Councillor in the Supreme Council of Pondicherry. Dupleix left for India in 1722. His preferential treatment at once attracted the mistrust of Governor Lenoir, and he was obliged to relinquish office. It took considerable influential protection from France, especially from his older brother, for him to hold on to any post. In Pondicherry, he learned to keep a low profile and to conduct business through a combination of intrigue and behind the scenes connections. These were to come in handy in 1731 when he was appointed director of the Chandernagor trading post. His tenure there was a success, as trade in Chandernagor increased significantly during his administration. He is alleged to have enriched himself immensely, thanks to the private business deals that the Company allowed its agents to conduct. Tales of his

Below: Government House circa 1755 by Dumont. CAOM DFC 33A80. ©CAOM Aix-en-Provence.

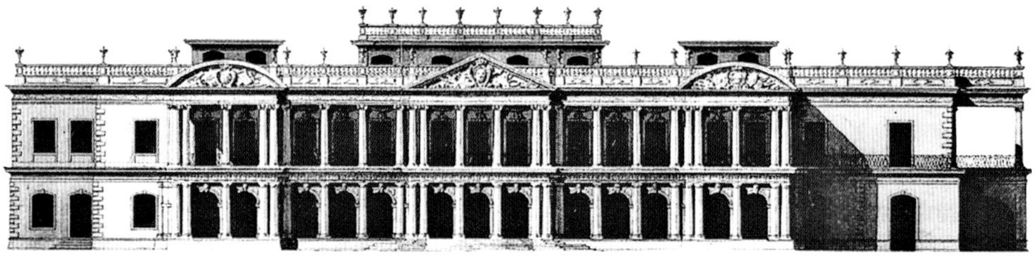

fabulous Chandernagor house and gardens spread, even to France. In 1741, he married the widow of his associate and friend; Jeanne Vincent, née De Castro, was a 'hat-donning Creole' who became a key influence upon Dupleix's career.

Dupleix's success did not go unnoticed by the Company. In 1742, on the departure of Governor Dumas, who had never appreciated him, he was finally appointed governor of Pondicherry. Along with his wife of Indo-Portuguese background, he brought a new vision of European trade and introduced a new approach to the balance of power in India by openly engaging himself in political games. He acquired the title of Nawab of Pondicherry and soon the company was able to collect a significant income from its huge *jagirs*, those fiscal seigneuries attributed by the Mughals to the Nawabs. In 1746, according to an anonymous witness: 'Everyday, when he leaves home, he is preceded by two flags and an escort of a dozen mounted guards who accompany him, particularly when he goes out of town. But when he

Above: Governor Bonvin and the flag of Dupleix, found in a warehouse by Gabriel Jouveau-Dubreuil in 1945.

Right: Governor Dupleix by Sergent Antoine Louis François. Reproduction of the original published in *Le Petit Journal*, late 19th century.

marches in ceremony, he is preceded by more than a hundred troopers and three elephants, upon which his flags are carried, and his coach is followed by a crowd of horsemen and jesters.'

This 'nawabism' saw the growing Indianisation of the French presence, a logical consequence of trading treaties negotiated with local princes, and of the remoteness of decision-makers, which led to the virtual autonomy of the trading posts. The Company could overlook these developments as long as profits continued to fill the coffers. Business success depended on the *dubash*, the big Indian business brokers. The diaries of Ananda Ranga Pillai, Dupleix's official interpreter and broker, clearly indicate the extent of Indian control of trade on behalf of the French. His house, facing the Grand Bazaar, remains a rare vestige of the eighteenth century in modern Pondicherry, and reflects the power and wealth of this man, whose diary constitutes a unique document of the French period.

Meanwhile, the clash of different European mercantile interests in India was increasing. Under Dupleix's leadership, as competition strengthened, French

Right: Plan of Pondicherry town, citadel, forts and surroundings by engineer Sornay, dated 14 October 1753, along with the project for a citadel to the south of the town. CAOM, Aix-en-Provence, CAOM DFC 32 B 55.

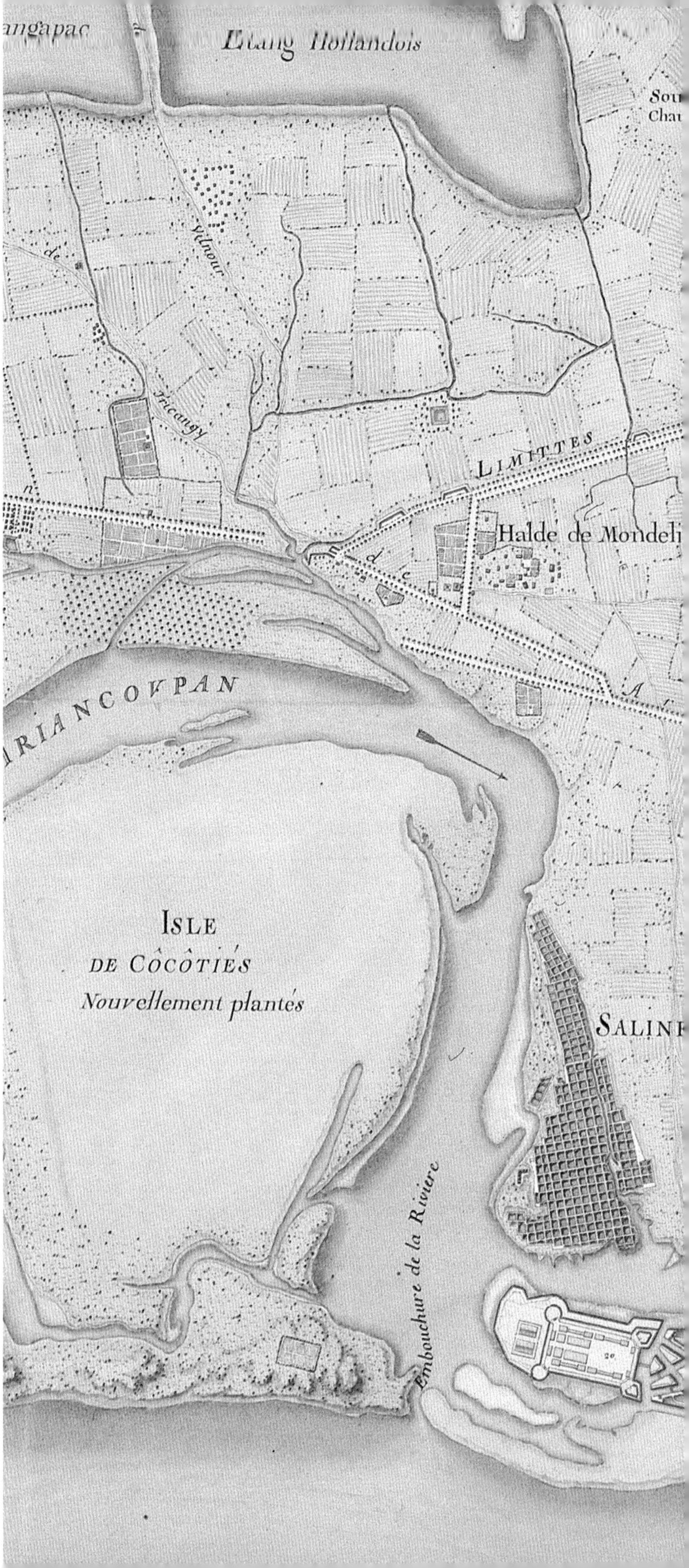

Chauderie d'Ellapa
Halde Ellapapote
Chemin
Chemin
Chauderie Permance
LIMITTES
Halde Paquemorean Pactou
Parcherie
Parcherie
Halde de Caucepaleon
Halde Charon
Emplacement de l'Hôpital
Allée de l'Etoille
Moutalepate

Left: 'View of the marvellous swing in the Pondicherry Governor's garden', anonymous lithograph circa 1750. This imaginary picture bears testimony to the idealisation of the city's power during the 18th century.

Below: View of Pondicherry in the middle of the 18th century. This engraving, of English origin, presents an imaginary Pondicherry reconstructed from descriptions and plans. It reveals the power and beauty that was attributed to the French trading post in its golden age.

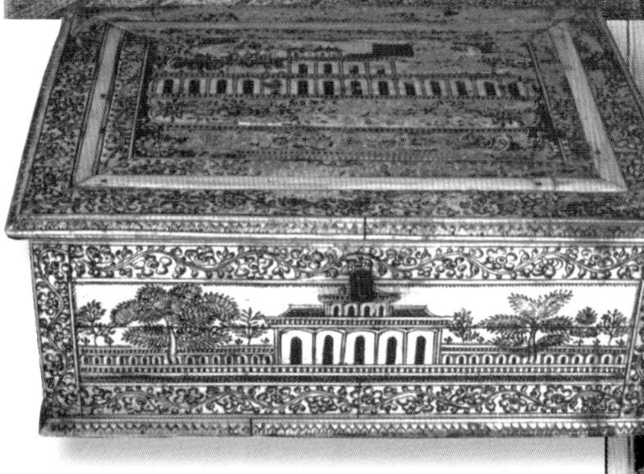

Above:
Ivory box, 18th century.
Pondicherry Museum, Pic. © IFP.

attitudes hardened. Madras, the first British establishment in the region, and only a 150 kilometres away from Pondicherry, refused to come to any agreement with the French concession. As early as the 1740s, the experience of colonial rivalry provoked rising nationalism. Sometime after 1750, one of the directors of the British East India Company in Madras, comments, 'It is more and more obvious that the French first want to squeeze the English out of the Coromandel trade, and later from India itself.' Among the Europeans in India, usually reasonably courteous among themselves, hostilities came into the open. The situation in Europe also deteriorated, and by the outbreak of the War of the Austrian Succession in 1746, it became obvious that the contest between France and Britain was no longer limited to the European arena, but was now officially worldwide. Dupleix was unaware of a third area of competition within France itself, in which interests in the West and East Indies were in opposition: American trade in sugar and slaves was generating higher financial returns than Indian trade in textiles, spices and precious stones. By the close of the eighteenth century, Saint Domingue alone represented over half of French foreign trade.

Right: Tiruvengadam III, Ananda Ranga Pillai's nephew. He held the post of *dubash* for a few years.

Tropical Battles and Trading Posts under Siege

The situation called for strong political direction and Dupleix rose to the occasion. In 1746, he attacked and captured Madras, taking advantage of the presence of a naval squadron from Bourbon Island commanded by Mahé de La Bourdonnais. However, La Bourdonnais' fleet was scattered by a hurricane and he signed a treaty ensuring the return of Madras to the English at the end of hostilities. To a furious Dupleix, he replied: 'You wanted Madras, I gave it to you with the agreement to surrender it, it is true. If that is not acceptable, you can go ahead and break the treaty.' The victory at Madras and the superb defence of Pondicherry in 1748 showed the strength of the French presence. But it increased tenfold the competition between the French and the British. Furthermore, even when the War of the Austrian Succession ended and Madras was returned to the British in exchange for Louisburg, hostilities did not end, but were carried on within the arena of Indian politics.

During a succession dispute between the ruler of Hyderabad, Nasir Jang, and his nephew Muzzafar Jang in league with the pretender of Arcot, Chanda Sahib, Dupleix chose to take the side of the plaintiff. The conspiracy triumphed thanks to the conquest of Gingee in 1750 and a victorious campaign by the French. Dupleix obtained Muzaffar from the Deccan's new Soubab (administrator) and Chanda Sahib, the new Nawab of Arcot, granted him extensive privileges. Dupleix was appointed troop commander of the kingdom of Arcot and extended the control of Pondicherry to include the village of Villianur. Through Joseph Patissier de Bussy-Castelnau, his lieutenant, who became resident to the Nizam of Hyderabad, he ruled the entire Deccan plateau. It was at this time that Dupleix began to take on the airs of a true nawab and build himself a magnificent palace.

Meanwhile, the Raja of Tanjore, a bad paymaster and little-inclined to submission, tried to bring down Chanda Sahib, the Nawab of Arcot, with the help of the British who supported Mehemet Ali, a pretender to Chanda Sahib's throne. The military campaigns, short-lived but extremely violent, went against the French who failed to unseat Mehemet Ali from his fortress in Trichinopoly. There was a spate of assassinations and deaths in India. In 1751, the Nizam of Hyderabad was killed, but his uncle was installed in his place. When the Marathas entered the fray, Bussy was forced to support this puppet king.

Opposite: The last days of French India. In 1761, the town is surrounded by the English forces, and led to surrender. Early 20th century lithograph.

In 1753, Chanda Sahib, the Nawab of Arcot, was captured in Srinagar and summarily executed. Confronted by the young British officer Robert Clive, the French began to back down and eventually participate in negotiations.

By year's end, it became obvious that the attempt to consolidate French influence over South India had failed. War and disputes with Indian kings had left the French colony in a state of ruin. Dupleix was summoned back to France to render accounts and he was judged severely. Jean-Louis-Xavier de Boisserolle, representing officers whom Dupleix had accused of incompetence, argued, 'Why, while he was sacrificing the king's subjects to his frenzied ambition and drawing their blood to fill his coffers with gold and diamonds, was he not ever tempted to lead these daredevil expeditions himself?'

Opposite page: Pondicherry in 1760. This is one of the two existing views of Pondicherry in the 18th century; it was by an Indian artist, obviously impressed by the rather huge mass of bricks that made up the defences of the town. Tanjore Museum.

Right: Portrait of Lally-Tollendal before his execution on 9 May 1766, when he is reported to have said: 'I commend my memory to my son and I die without a grudge.'

A direct consequence of this fiasco was the extreme timidity shown by subsequent governors towards Indian politics and the attempt to respect Company instructions, which stated that war was detrimental to commercial interests. But events took a turn for the worse with the outbreak of the Seven Years' War in 1756. A squadron sent out under the command of Lally-Tollendal, an Irish Catholic who had emigrated to France to escape religious persecution, was not provided sufficient arms by the French king. The British were determined to throw the French out without fear of Indian reprisals. In 1757, they captured Chandernagor. Lally-Tollendal, the Governor of Pondicherry, retaliated by destroying Fort Saint David in 1758 and then dispatching all his troops to take Madras, thus following in Dupleix's footsteps. The siege proved a complete fiasco and Lully was defeated at Vandavasi in 1760. In his obsession with Dupleix, he overlooked the defence of Pondicherry, which was besieged for a year, reduced to starvation and finally captured by the English in 1761. Lord Pigot, a French Protestant who served the East Indian Company, ordered the 'white' town razed to the ground in reprisal for the destruction

MÉMOIRE
PRODUIT
AU CONSEIL D'ÉTAT
DU ROI,
PAR TROPHIME-GERARD, COMTE DE LALLY-TOLENDAL, Capitaine de Cavalerie au Régiment des Cuiraffiers, dans l'Inftance en caffation de l'Arrêt du 6 Mai 1766, qui a condamné à mort le feu Comte DE LALLY fon pere, Lieutenant Général des Armées du Roi, &c.
ET SIGNIFIÉ POUR DÉFENSE
A ROUEN,
M. DCC. LXXIX.

PIECES JUSTIFICATIVES
A.
MONSIEUR,

RÉFUTATION
DES FAITS IMPUTÉS
Au Sieur GODEHEU
PAR
Le Sieur DUPLEIX.

Below: Memos presented in court defending the position of governors between 1754-1774.

Left:
Plan of the second battle of Vandavasi and the siege of Pondicherry in 1760.

Above:
Cannon used in the British campaign.

Left:
Bijapur sword.

of Fort David. Lally-Tollendal was taken prisoner, and sent to France where he was duly tried and executed in 1766 although he was posthumously rehabilitated following a campaign by Voltaire in 1778.

In 1773, the widow of the Company Surgeon Auber finally received legal acknowledgement of her claim on the loss of her house at the corner of the present Rue Suffren and Rue Lal Bahadur Shastri, in the form of a notarised document: 'After capturing the town, the English chased away all the inhabitants without exception and set about a systematic destruction of all fortifications and other buildings belonging to the Compagnie des Indes Orientales. They reduced churches and private houses to piles of rubble. Monsieur Auber's house

Right: Le Gentil's 1779 edition of *Voyage dans les Mers de l'Inde*. A scientist who set out in 1760, Le Gentil was unable to observe the passage of Venus in front of the sun in Pondicherry due to an overcast sky, and so decided to stay on in Asia for its second passage in 1769. Once again, he failed to observe it. Although he had left France supposedly for two years, he returned after a gap of thirteen years, when everyone back home thought him dead.

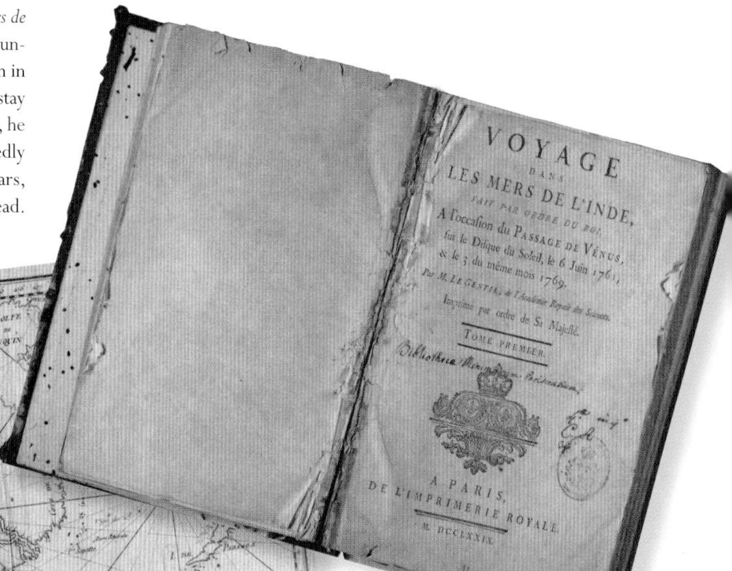

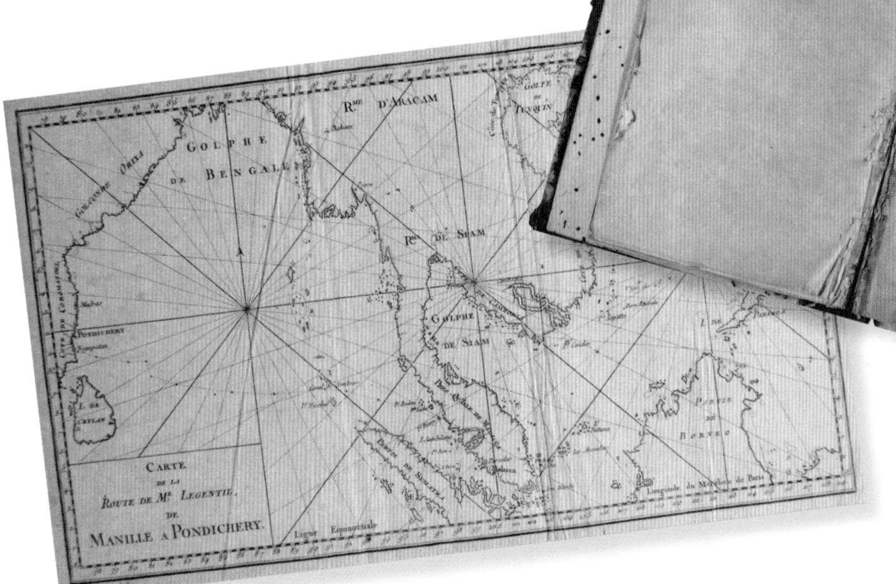

Left: Le Gentil's route from Manila to Pondicherry in 1769.

suffered the same fate.' Then too, 'the English removed from there all lumber, woodwork, doors, windows, fittings and generally all that which could be taken, excepting the rubble.'

The year 1761 was a turning point. Nevertheless 'the French adventure' had demonstrated to all the European states that when political unrest breaks out in a colonial hinterland, it is vital to retain control over the production and supply chain. In this way, other colonising nations of the nineteenth century benefitted from the tough lessons learned by the French East India Company.

Below: 'View of a part of the ruins of Pondicherry in 1769', plate produced in Le Gentil's *Voyage dans les Mers de l'Inde*. It is a unique testimonial of the destruction of Pondicherry and its difficult recovery.

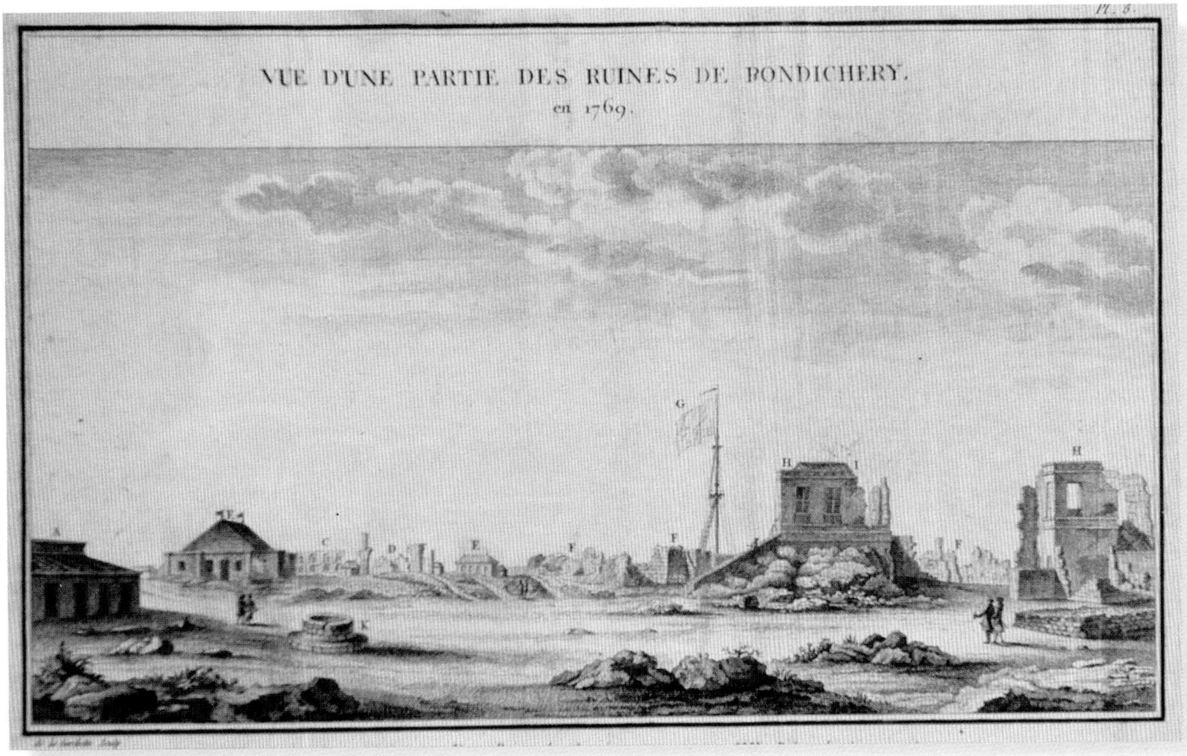

After the East Indies Rush

Razed to the ground in 1761, besieged again in 1778 and, despite Governor Bellecombe's brave defence, captured, Pondicherry was occupied by the English for a third time in 1793 during the French Revolution. The destruction of the French fleets in Aboukir Bay in 1796, and in 1805 at Trafalgar, prevented Revolutionary France and the Empire from lending any assistance to the trading posts. It was only under the Restoration that aid returned to the distant outpost.

On board the *Amphitrite*, Count Dupuy, sent by Louis XVIII as Governor in 1816, already knew that the golden age of the eighteenth century was a thing of the past, and that the Indian trading posts, isolated and scattered, were weaker than ever.

What could Dupuy expect from Pondicherry? Very little, apart from following his instructions to quietly re-establish order so as to govern in peace in an India under British administration. Large-scale trade was almost out of the question. Lorient, Nantes and Bordeaux had already turned the page on the Indian trading posts, although it would not be long before Marseille would show interest. Pondicherry itself turned into a small rural colony and the trading posts became 'administrative establishments' (Établissements Français en Inde).

Opposite page: Review of Sepoys in Government Square in Pondicherry, circa 1825 (early 19th-century watercolour). Government House was reconstructed around 1765 by the engineer Bourcet on the foundations of the Hôtel de la Compagnie des Indes.

A Hopeless Bargain

Dupuy arrived to find an almost deserted town, here described by a British officer, Lieutenant-Colonel Fraser: 'Ever since we took possession of Pondicherry, almost all the public buildings have fallen to ruin.' Furthermore, the conditions for handing back the French trading posts, set out in the Treaty of Paris (1814) at the putative end of the Napoleonic Wars, were very restrictive: the disarmament of the trading posts, the prohibition of any sort of military garrison or rebuilding of fortifications and the recovery of a few villages around Pondicherry, of unclear and ill-defined boundaries, which had been under French control prior to 1793. The British were very precise; anything on high ground would be British, and only low-lying land, French. Britain also reserved for itself the profits from the opium trade in Chandernagor and took over the salt works of Pondicherry to retain its monopoly on key products. On the other hand, significant compensation was paid to the colony, 'India's one million', a significant amount of money, plus a certain amount of opium. And yet, we read in a French document of 1840: 'I know for sure that war itself is round the corner and that if it breaks out, we would have to be

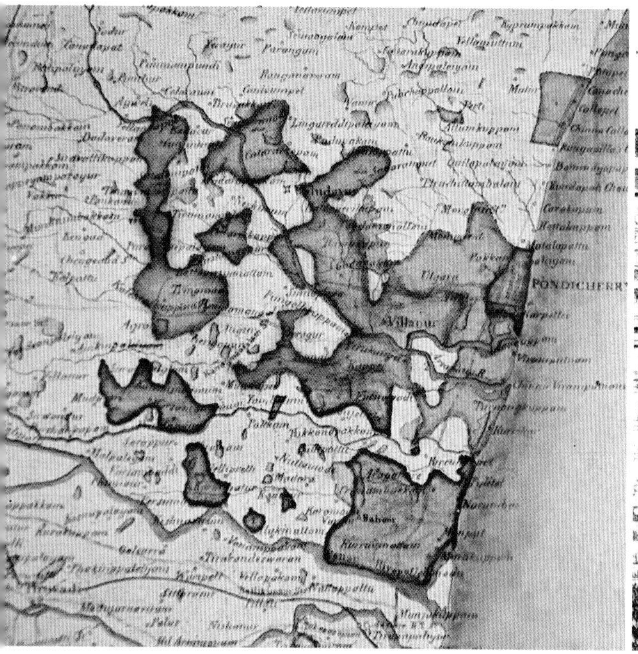

ready to pack our bags and leave according to the agreed stipulations.'

But if the formal conditions for handing back the trading posts in 1814 were harsh, the actual transfer was even harsher. The return of the establishments was done ungraciously and the British authorities handed power back to the French a year later than stipulated. Madras also imposed a British Resident. The village dependencies of Pondicherry were returned only due to the Governor's insistence and the British took advantage of their fuzzy drawing of borders to appropriate the best plots of land. The final layout of the French territory was more like a piece of tattered cloth, the holes isolated from one another. The Madras Presidency levied a 16 per cent tax on the produce of these zones at the borders, which made any economic development of the French

Opposite left: Map of French possessions (in violet) in the Pondicherry district, late 19th century, modern colours.

Opposite right: View of the Canal, circa 1830. Started around 1770, it was completed in 1827.

Below: European ships at sea on the Coromandel coast, circa 1825. Fishermen and boatmen. Hand-coloured lithograph.

enclaves almost impossible. The authorities of French India responded by declaring the port of Pondicherry exempt from all taxes. Pondicherry could breathe again, albeit feebly: 'A Danish and an American ship, having learnt that no taxes had to be paid, dropped anchor at this harbour and unloaded a whole cargo, which was then transported on donkeys to Goudelour and Ceylon.' Meanwhile, however, metropolitan France required all traded goods to pass via Marseille, even though the trade might be carried out directly from colony to colony. The French Exchequer also appropriated 'India's one million'; the colony would not benefit from it until 1931. In such dire circumstances, the local French administration imposed a 50 per cent tax on all agricultural produce, putting farmers under enormous pressure.

Thus France in India was reduced to a silent presence with little or no *raison d'être* either in the eyes of the British or of metropolitan France. Several times in the course of the nineteenth century, the French were tempted to negotiate territorial exchanges, even considering the sale of Pondicherry to the highest bidder. In the end, however, both sides accepted the status quo; it was left to the Indian farmer to pay the price of colonial rivalry.

Two important factors changed Franco-British relations in mid-century. The first was the rise to power of Napoleon III in France in 1851, followed by the Sepoy Mutiny in 1857, which led to the abolition of the British East India Company and the creation of the British Raj. From then on, the draconian British rules were slowly lifted in Pondicherry. The second critical factor was the revived interest in the role of the colonies. In 1830, Charles X, seeking to occupy his troops, ordered an expedition to Algeria and set up a permanent presence there. The Second Empire encouraged the extension of the Algerian conquest and the despatch of expeditionary forces to China and Mexico. Between 1858 and 1867, with the conquest and annexation of Cochinchina, the departure-point for the colonisation of Indo-China, Pondicherry regained its strategic importance as the gateway to the East. French India would no longer be the last link in the colonial chain. With this gradual extension of its empire, France could no longer afford to neglect its old colonies. Administrative procedures were analysed, codified and organised according to periodically-updated regulations from the early 1850s.

Opposite page: Races organised during the celebration of festivals on 12 August 1863 at the Government Square.

A World in Itself

With the return of the French, colonial society in the 'white' township was re-established and many colonial houses were constructed at the beginning of the nineteenth century. All that remained of the old fort was a sun scorched open space, which occasionally served as a military parade ground. After an initial period of apathy and corruption, the return of French civil servants revitalised this community, composed essentially of Creole descendants of the merchants of the golden age. The foundation of a colonial school in 1826 was followed by a public library in 1827 and a colonial hospital in 1858.

Picture the life-style of the French and the Creoles during this period. To start with, the white community was never very large, just over a thousand strong, of which only just over one hundred were 'metropolitan' French. The pace of life was determined by the climate. On the whole the French found it hard to adjust to the weather, especially during April and May. For them, 'Pondicherry is the ideal oven that Providence has offered to those who are sensitive to the cold. The sun is deadly; the slightest ray falling straight on a person for half a minute will destroy him more surely than a pistol shot.'

Background: View of the Pondicherry landing stage, circa 1835. Lithograph by Cabassol.

It became necessary to adapt to the pace of life and construct spacious dwellings with large 'verandas, high ceilings and large spaces'. This allowed a freer circulation of air, but these homes were not constructed in the Tamil style for an extended family. If the first enemy for the colonials was the blistering sun, the second enemy was boredom and isolation. Inhabitants all knew one another's business, and any newcomer was scrutinised with intense curiosity in a town short of distractions. 'In the courtyards or under the verandas of their house,' a witness explains, 'they set up tables for games and the first person to arrive, provided he was of European extraction, entered, introduced himself and without much ado settled down to a game of bouillotte.' But the most popular entertainment remained dancing and dinner receptions. They were sometimes organised by rich European businessmen, sometimes by Indians. Perhaps the most elaborate reception was one hosted by a Tamil merchant, Arounassalom Sabapady, who having invited the best and most illustrious members of Pondicherry society, did not actually deign to meet and mix with them. Louis Charolais, private secretary to Governor de Verninac, gives a tongue-in-cheek observation of a reception in 1852: 'After an hour of gambolling to music, everybody was dripping wet. One might be forgiven for mistaking them for a group of Poseidon's Tritons and Nereids.'

Hearsay and rumour thrived. While the men gathered in closed circles to

Relaxed life on the east side of the canal

Opposite page: In the 19th century, French houses took on once again the characteristics of private residences constructed in the 18th century. Usually a floor was added. Above the colonnaded porticos, large corridors opened on to a garden. Straight, long balconies made it possible to enjoy the sea breeze. The flat terrace, called *argamasse* by the French, allowed one to have the benefit of the cool of the evening. The whole building was enclosed by a high, wide wall, pierced by an entrance with a shape and design that indicated the social status of its owner. A house on Rue François Martin.

Left and above: A palanquin, early 19th century. Passengers rented these at the landing stage along with porters; the whole contraption is called a *bouée*.

Above: An official ceremony in May 1835.
Lithograph by Sigismond Himely, 1836.
National Library of Australia.

smoke and play in private, the women visited one another to exchange books and precious gossip. Some took to writing short stories, tales about what they considered to be Indian culture. However, contacts between Indians and French were usually restricted to a minimum, limited largely to the domestic staff that worked in 'white' town households. These included butlers, housemaids and man servants, fan *wallahs*, or chair and palanquin carriers. Outings were planned to lakes in the countryside and trips were organised to British hill-stations. Louis de Charolais describes the Oussoudou lake: 'I have never seen a more pleasant sight than all these small boats furrowing the vastness of this tranquil lake, all colourfully decorated and mirrored in the clear waters.'

But the disparity between the colony and metropolitan France was so marked, that when the Viceroy of British India the Prince of Wales, visited Chandernagor in 1885, the reporter of the newspaper *Le Temps* wrote mockingly about his compatriots, commenting that 'you could see here some splendid examples of 1830s fashions!' In any case, colonial dress-styles remained extremely different from those of Indians. In order to emphasise their difference, or out of loyalty to their home culture, colonials continued to wear European clothes well into the 1900s. They wore heavy suits made of thick cloth, with double-breasted jackets for the men and crinoline dresses and petticoats for the ladies. Dress was the ultimate sign of cultural and social belonging and the Indian style of dress was a privilege that was reserved for the half-breed. A common belief held that heat, indolence and contact with Indians would lead to crime!

Though tending to be superficial and provincial, French settlement society produced some interesting exceptions. A number of scholars and distinguished scientists resided in Pondicherry and pioneered in French exposure to Indian culture. Following in the footsteps of Pierre Poivre, Anquetil-Duperron and Sonnerat, who were representative of the eighteenth-century Enlightenment, Edmond Ariel and, later, Julien Vinson revived French studies of South Indian culture. In 1828, the botanist George Perrotet established the Botanical Garden of Pondicherry, creating an extensive laboratory for the adaptation of plants such as vanilla, coffee, tea and sugarcane to local conditions.

Left: French officer of the Pondicherry garrison, circa 1863. Lithograph.

Below: The common cat of India owes its scientific name (*Felix jacquemontis*) to Victor Jacquemont, the great traveller and naturalist. Supplement to the *Travels of Victor Jacquemont*, circa 1830.

Right:
India's Common Chameleon
by Victor Jacquemont.

Above:
The bayadere (temple dancers) of Pondicherry.
Lithograph by Sigismond Himely,
1836, modern colouring.
National Library of Australia.

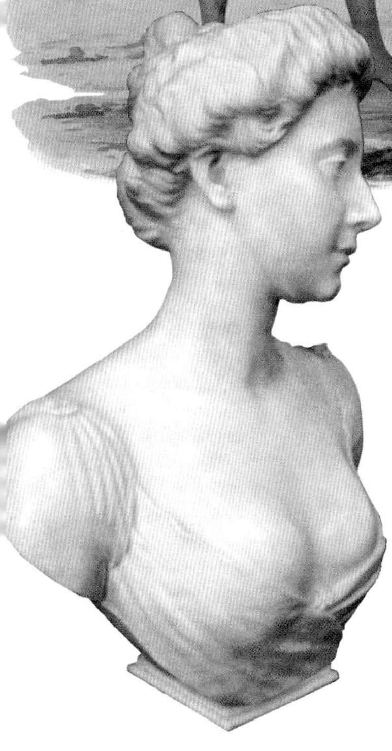

Left: Bust of a beautiful French lady in Pondicherry. Marble bust, beginning 20th century, anonymous.

A Bastion of Hinduism

There were other scholars interested in the rituals, history and religion of South India, indologists such as Eugène Burnouf and Eugène Jacquet whose accounts triggered the first craze for India in France. The eighteenth century fondness for voyages of discovery continued into the nineteenth century and Pondicherry became a compulsory stopover. *La Thétis* arrived in 1824, followed by *La Favorite* in 1830 and *La Bonite* around 1836. Names, some long since forgotten, such as Victor Jacquemont, Émile Guimet and Pierre Loti feature among visitors to Pondicherry during the century. This stream of travellers, intrigued by India, paved the way for setting up two institutions which still exist, the Institut Français d'Indologie and the École Française d'Extrême-Orient.

In Pondicherry, travellers discovered and studied a society whose workings were so different that often its rules and traditional values appeared incomprehensible to the European mind. Religious traditions, however, constituted the core of Indian life, a fact which French administrators could ignore only at their peril. As the historian Jacques Weber stated: 'Though he is capable of tolerating all kinds of deprivations, is capable of enduring the worst sufferings without complaint or revolt, the Indian snaps out of his torpor and forgets his natural sweetness at the slightest violation of his customs and rituals, to which he is ferociously attached above everything.' It was for this reason that one of the first acts of Governor Dupuy, in 1819, was to reaffirm the underlying principles of the French presence: 'Indians, whether Christian, Moor or Gentile, will be judged as in the past, according to the laws, customs and rituals of their respective caste.'

In the 'black' town, Hinduism was predominant. The main population was Shivaite and in 1824, there were five big temples and eighteen smaller pagodas (*pagotins*). During the year, festivals succeed one another, and processions going from one area to another trace a religious and social demarcation reflecting hierarchy and precedence. In January, there is Pongal or the end of the monsoon, and the harvesting of staple rice. Then come Thaipusam and Shivaratri, the darkest night of Shiva. In the month of February, Pondicherry celebrates the festival of venomous snakes, and of the cobra, in particular. In May, on the day of the new moon, the festival of the great temple of Villianur takes place, when the procession of great 'juggernaut' carts are pulled by hand over several kilometres. September sees the celebration of the birthday of the elephant-

Opposite: View of a temple in Pondicherry. Early 19th century lithograph by Sigismond Himely, modern colouring. National Library of Australia.

god Ganesh, followed by Ayudhyapuja, or the festival of arms and tools, which is held near the Grand Bazaar. In October, Diwali commemorates Rama's victory over the Asuras and the liberation of Sita. It is also the time to honour ancestors by performing sacrifices and offering new clothes to family members. Finally, the festival of Karthikai celebrates the victory of Shiva and his sons over evil.

If most of these public ceremonies were accepted and even encouraged, there were others, restricted to the lower castes, whose religious fervour shocked the Europeans. On the last day of the Fire Festival at Dupuypet, bare-footed penitents cross a bed of burning coals, especially prepared for the occasion. At Veerampattinam, Pattanava fishermen frequently celebrate the festival of Mariamman, the goddess of smallpox. In order to assure an abundant catch, penitent fishermen are suspended from the thirty-foot high mast of an outrigger by a hook embedded in their skin. However, it was rare for anyone to die from these rituals, and rumours of religious suicides often resulted from exaggerated reports of accidents. *Sati*, the cremation of a widow on her husband's pyre, was unknown in Pondicherry.

The 'black' town of early nineteenth century Pondicherry was made up of three distinct categories of Hindus. The Brahmins who were either temple priests and gurus (religious teachers) dedicated

Below: 'A Brahmin's Marriage', coloured lithograph, early 19th century. The marriage ceremony is one of the most important and codified rituals in Indian society.

Right:
The Governor Saint-Simon (1835-1840), known as a defensor of the interests of the Indians in Pondicherry, is depicted in an Indian outfit. The Pondicherry lighthouse, visible in the background, was erected during his governorship.

Around the Grand Bazaar

Right: Rangani was a Telugu-speaking palanquin-carrier. The job was so exhausting that it was rare for a carrier to work for several seasons at a stretch.

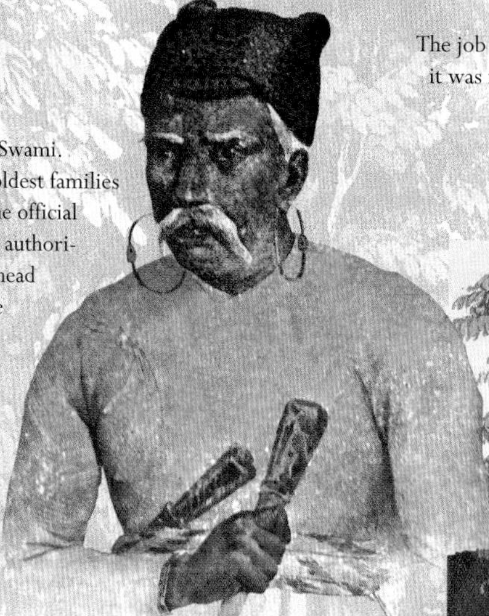

Right: Portrait of Nalla Swami. Hailing from one of the oldest families of Pondicherry, he was the official interpreter of the French authorities. A Christian, he was head of his caste, and therefore carries a cane topped with a golden apple, and a dagger attached to his belt.

Above: Portrait of Latchimi, aged 45, circa 1824. A low-caste woman, she was a midwife by profession. Very competent, she was equally in demand among the Indians and Europeans in Pondicherry, which explains her rich jewellery.

Above: View of the Grand Bazaar of Pondicherry, founded by Governor Desbassyn de Richemont in 1827. 1836 lithograph. National Library of Australia.

Right: Portrait of Virapattiren, *sadhu* (holy man) and devotee of Shiva.

Left: Adjagu Tannir Karichy, 'the beautiful water-carrier'. Of very low caste, she often worked as a maid in European households.

Left: Mouttouvira Soupraya was a Vellala, devoted to Shiva. His father, Ramalinga, was a farmer on the king's estate and in charge of supplying Lally-Tollendal's army. In 1761, under siege in Kanjivaram fort, he is said to have loaded the cannons at his own cost. The French administration had still not reimbursed his son in 1824.

Left: Santusa. Between 45 and 50 years old in 1824, he sat every day in the Grand Bazaar where he worked as a money-changer.

Above: Kammatachi, the bayadere. Between 28 and 30 years old, she had arrived in Pondicherry in 1824 for the wedding of the great provost. She wears the *tali* round her neck as a symbol of her sacred union with God.

to the study of the *Vedas*, or interpreters, writers and civil servants. The Shudras, the numerically dominant caste in town, were comprised of two main communities – the Vellalas, who no doubt originated from the countryside, were bankers or businessmen noted for their intellect and culture, and the Chettiars, who, on the other hand, had controlled large-scale trade since the eighteenth century. There were also several other Shudra castes engaged in business in Pondicherry. The Komuttis were grocers and jewellers; the Kavarais, Senaikkudaiyars, the Maleamans or Vanniyars were oil merchants. Others, like the Reddis, were landowners, while the Pallis were labourers, craftsmen and weavers, considered by the Brahmins to be of a low caste. The third category of Hindus consisted of outcastes including manufacturers of *kallu* or coconut alcohol, the bayaderes or Devadasis, dancers attached to a temple, whose children, the palanquin carriers, were called Boyis, Boy or Boë. There were also potters, fishermen and boatmen called Pattanava or Makkuvan; hunters, barbers, laundrymen, the Kuravas, often described as Indian gypsies, jugglers and musicians; and the Tottis, the garbage collectors.

Opposite page: View of the interior of a temple in Pondicherry, 19th century lithograph (1836). National Library of Australia.

Finally there were the Pariahs, organised into thirteen subdivisions, who were reproached, among other things, for their promiscuity with Europeans. As the 1819 edict of Governor Dupuy testifies, caste practices were far from being limited only to the Hindu populations; with Christians and Muslims following many of the same rituals.

Even though rigidly organised into endogamous groups, society in the 'black' township still experienced social tensions. Contrary to what Europeans might imagine, social hierarchy in India was not fixed, but rather depended on custom, respect for religious strictures by communities and sometimes, even on financial success. Thus, a caste which is looked down upon, can very well, with time, gain respect. For example, the Vellalas and the Chettiars of Pondicherry aspired to the Vaishya caste, whilst some communities with higher aspirations, adopted the distinctive signs of other castes to advertise their new social status. In South India, for at least one hundred years, these oppositions were expressed as a form of conflict between the 'Right Hand' and the 'Left Hand'. Throughout the entire first half of the nineteenth century, the use of roads in the 'black' town was determined by an inhabitant belonging to one or the other 'Hand'.

In these circumstances, the French administrators were obliged to acknowledge the primacy of Hinduism in Pondicherry. In 1845, for instance, at the outbreak of a smallpox epidemic, the French wanted to shift the cremation ground to Karaikal, but this led to a revolt in which France almost lost the settlement. In 1848, in Kuruchikuppam, one of the suburbs of Pondicherry, riots broke out against the Pariahs, who evidently were convinced that the establishment of a Republic in France granted them the right to wear footwear, an emblem of the upper castes. Social peace depended upon religious peace, and this was traditionally purchased through Justice bowing to Custom. That is why Dupuy had reinstated the institutions of the Ancien Régime, reasserting the law of custom for native Indians, administered from the Tribunal de Chauderie in the nerve centre of the 'black' township, the Grand Bazaar.

In addition, each caste had its own internal tribunal. Supposedly under the jurisdiction of a Justice of the Peace, these institutions posed a delicate problem for French magistrates. It became necessary in 1827 to establish a Committee for Indian Jurisprudence which was the successor to a consultation chamber created in the eighteenth century. The Committee was made up of the leaders of the main castes and headed by an Indian, Tiruvingadapoulle, with the initial commission to draft a 'Code of Laws, Mores and Customs of Hindus on the Coromandel Coast'. When this was completed in 1840, the Committee became operational. However, the kind of law that was practised shocked more than one French jurist and often left Christians in a constant state of apoplexy. Arranged child- and consanguineous marriages were accepted, polygamy was tolerated and corporal punishment by caning was prevalent, leading to an infinitely worse fate than loss of caste.

The policy did prove successful in certain areas. In 1854, Governor de Verninac succeeded in declaring the roads freely open to all after making caste leaders accept that nowhere in the sacred texts could any justification for dividing society into 'Left' and 'Right' hand be found. But all these efforts up to the 1870s, were focussed on maintaining law and order and it was not until the Third Republic that more ambitious and sustainable policies emerged.

Right: Portrait of Vardapa, 45 years old, circa 1825. He was the head of the Mouchi caste (canvas painters) of Pondicherry. Here, he carries the cane topped with a golden head, in conformity with his status. Coloured lithograph, early 19th century.

A prominent citizen's house in the 'black' township in late 19th century

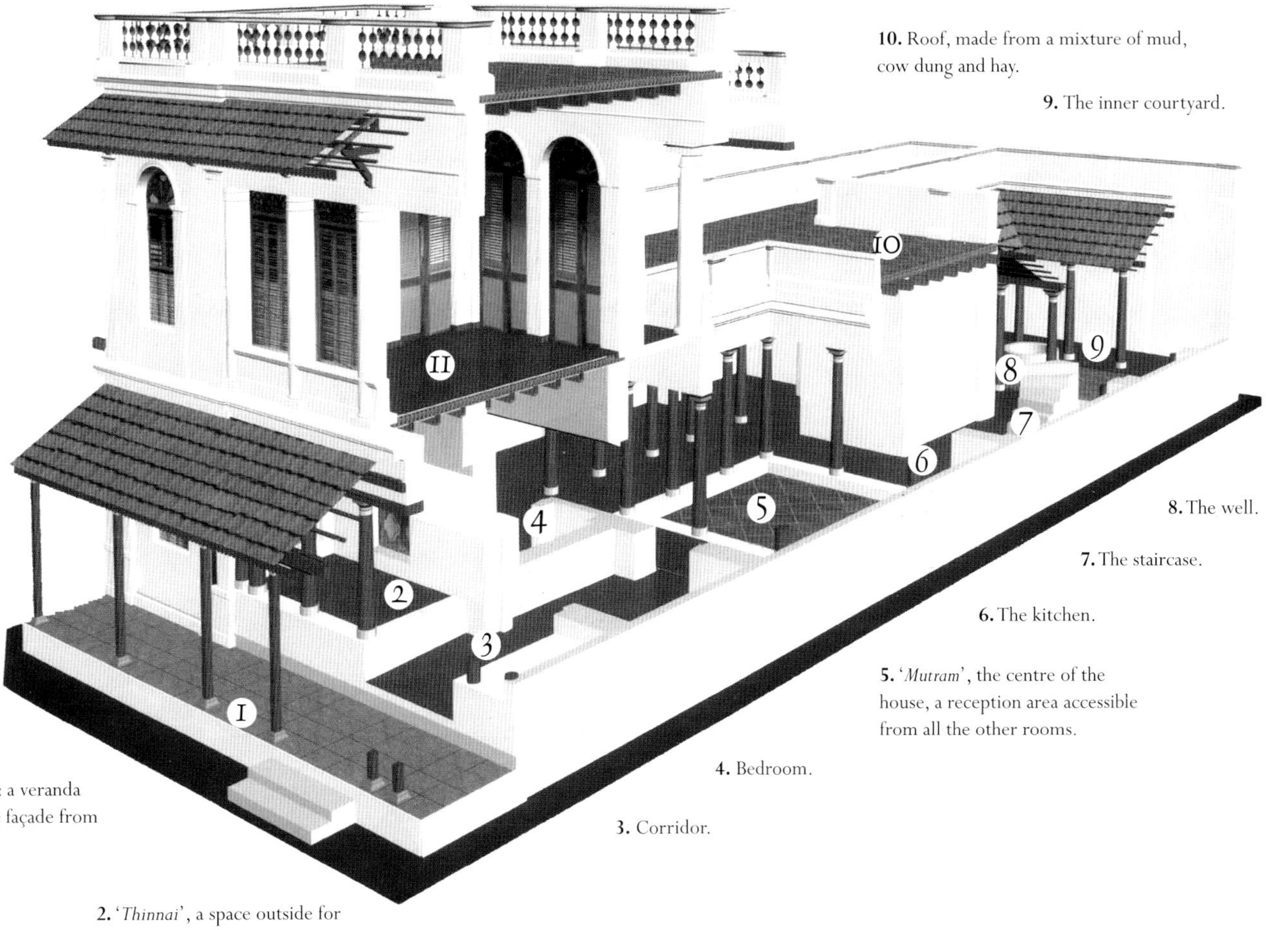

.'*Thalvaram*': a veranda
-otecting the façade from
-e sun.

2. '*Thinnai*', a space outside for resting, open to passers-by.

3. Corridor.

4. Bedroom.

5. '*Mutram*', the centre of the house, a reception area accessible from all the other rooms.

6. The kitchen.

7. The staircase.

8. The well.

9. The inner courtyard.

10. Roof, made from a mixture of mud, cow dung and hay.

11. Reception room and dining room.

Opposite page: The Indian house was the basis of all social life in the 'black' town. It sheltered the whole family and was also a place of work. It reflected the community and the social status of its residents. Unlike European houses, where light is let in through large windows designed to take full advantage of the cool sea breeze, the Indian house seeks shade, while being well ventilated by openings in the roof. The central room, called the *mutram*, is at once a meeting-place for residents and for guests of honour, and a place for washing oneself. A Muslim house on Kazy Street in Pondicherry.

Above: Portrait of Chahagaramusen, a Muslim born in Pondicherry. In 1758, he enlisted as a sepoy in Lally-Tollendal's army. When the French returned, in 1816, he was granted a pension, which he used for a pilgrimage to Mecca. Around 1824, when he had collected enough donations, he sought permission from the administration to build a mosque on the Madras road.

Coolie Trade

Around 1856, the Administrator, Saint-Hilaire, observed: 'Our settlements have experienced a sense of well-being for the last six to eight years, and this is due to emigration.' Though the colony had found itself in very difficult conditions between 1820 and 1856, France was now discovering that Indian emigration could play an important role in retaining its sugar trade. Since the end of the eighteenth century, an important part of foreign French wealth had been generated in the French Caribbean. A small number of colonists oversaw the work by slaves bought in by slave drivers on the African coast, particularly Gorée and Saint Louis in Senegal.

The French Revolution, of course, would not tolerate slavery which was first abolished in 1794, but then reinstated by Napoleon in 1803. The trade of slaves was forbidden by the Paris treaty of 1814. In 1830, when Victor Schœlcher, son of an Alsatian businessman, arrived in Cuba, he discovered the full horror of the

Below: A last glance at India before exile. The south end of the 'white' town seen from the lighthouse. Photograph, late 1860s. The warehouses intended for recruited coolies were located beyond the boulevards.

Below: Coolies or porters, coloured lithograph, early 19th century. They were of low caste and not well looked upon, which partly explains why they went overseas for work. For the French, any Indian who worked as a labourer was called a 'coolie'.

Below: Map of French settlements in India, circa 1850, published in *La France Pittoresque*.

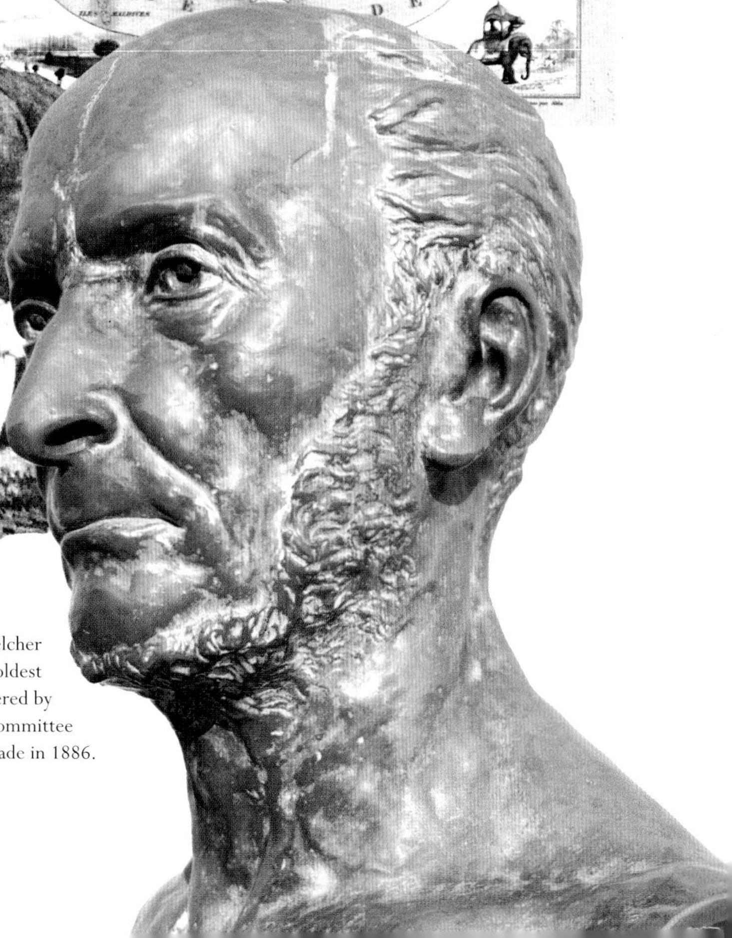

Right: Bust of Victor Schœlcher in Pondicherry. One of his oldest likenesses, it was ordered by a Pondicherry committee and made in 1886.

system. Appointed Under-Secretary for the Merchant Navy and the Colonies under the Second Republic in 1848, Schœlcher achieved the permanent abolition of slavery, to the despair of big landowners on the islands. However, the absence of any effective land reform meant that the benefits of abolition remained largely theoretical. Moreover, what hurt the big planters most was not so much the end of slavery but the end of the slave-trade. Confronted by growing competition from sugar beet, landowners were facing a shortage of labour.

New blood was to be found in India and it flowed out from Yanam, Pondicherry and Karaikal. 'The coolie is the perfect immigrant,' wrote one. 'This race is well-formed and robustly built, although refined and elegant too, easily acclimatised and of sweet and submissive nature, and distinguishes itself above all by its scrupulous sense of honour for commitments undertaken.' Following the thaw in Franco-British relations, the coolie recruiters could shift their attention to the French colonies. The activity which started in the early 1830s in La Réunion, was extended subsequently to the West Indies and Guyana. It was legally well-framed, subject to clear regulations and rested on the theoretical consent of the would-be migrant. The migrants left for a period of at least five years, with the guarantee of a regular salary and repatriation, but their contracts belonged to the landowner. The continued push for profit in the French West Indies meant that providing a substantial workforce at short notice became vital. In February of 1850, an association of migrants was formed in Pondicherry to keep a check on any abuse or misuse and it soon developed into a veritable cartel. Recruitment was facilitated by the impoverishment of the peasantry, hit hard by famine, debt and taxation. The French therefore started recruiting on a massive scale in British India, with the tacit complicity of the administration there. This traffic started to become so profitable that from 1837 Great Britain decided to organise transportation themselves from the ports of Calcutta, Bombay and Madras.

In reality, legal recruiting regulations were ignored more often than not by over-zealous recruiters. Between 1850 and 1860, when negotiations proved ineffective, they resorted to the use of *kallu* or coconut alcohol or drugs, resorting to the cane, or outright lying to overcome any strong resistance. Whole villages could be raided and emptied overnight, their inhabitants locked away in warehouses to the south of Pondicherry, then pushed into dinghies and finally dumped unceremoniously below decks on the big ships lying in wait.

'There are infants and women who relieve themselves in bed at night,' observed Governor D'Ubraye in May 1850. 'In addition to this, if one considers that these ships had neither portholes nor scuttles, one can only imagine the kind of accidents and threats to life that prevailed in the pitch dark sleeping compartments below.' Nevertheless, the conditions of transport were, in general, considered satisfactory. On some ill-favoured ships, the mortality rate could exceed seven per cent. Scurvy and, above all, epidemics – in particular smallpox and cholera – were ruthless killers on the ships. But after the 1861 Franco-British convention, recruitments as well as travel conditions were quickly improved and the number of emigrants increased exponentially.

When they finally arrived in La Réunion or in Guyana, the Tamils were treated more like slaves than free workers and their contracts were often not honoured. Poor working conditions remained the principal cause of death among them. In the case of Martinique, Victor Schœlcher remarked: 'Is it not a criminal social state where a population, instead of increasing according to the laws of nature, loses, in twenty-two years, one third of its members?' So it was that over a hundred thousand people were shipped before the coolie trade came to an end in 1889.

Right:
A Vaishya organising a shipment. Coloured lithograph, early 19th century. Plate from *L'Inde française ou collection de dessins lithographiés* by E. Burnouf and E. Jacquet, 1835.

Oppposite page:
View of the Canal, lithograph by Sigismond Himely after Pâris, circa 1835. National Library of Australia.

167

The Opening up of French India and Economic Renewal

This sudden new prosperity in the second half of the nineteenth century was accompanied by important changes in the colony, many of them linked to the development of new means of communication and the power of industrialisation.

Thus, in less than a decade, Pondicherry came significantly closer to France. This was partly due to a rapid transformation of the navy between 1850 and 1860. At the beginning of the century, vessels required sails and were built entirely of wood. Now with advances in the steel industry, steel became the essential component of hulls, and, with the introduction of the steam engine, navigation became increasingly less dependent on the vagaries of wind power. Large steamers appeared on the principal maritime routes. Strategic inter-oceanic canals were being dug. The Suez Canal, opened in 1869, reduced the length of the journey considerably. From nearly eight months in the eighteenth century, Pondicherry, at the end of the nineteenth, was only two months away. A national ocean-liner company, the Messageries Impériales, was set up in 1851 to ensure regular links with the colonies. They operated between Pointe de Galles and Pondicherry from 1862 onward and in 1871 the company was renamed Messageries Maritimes. By contrast, the development of railways, which could have opened up the hinterland of Pondicherry, proved less than easy. The British refused to lay a coastal line and were more interested in developing a railway network towards Madurai than in helping the economic prosperity of Pondicherry, their old rival. 'Some people think it pointless to build a railway line connecting Madras to Nagapattinam via Pondicherry,' was a common refrain. After years of negotiations, the station was finally inaugurated in Pondicherry in 1879, linking it with Villupuram. Along with advances in transportation, came progress in communications, due in no large part to improved relations with Great Britain. The telegraph was installed in 1856 on a British network, allowing captains on long sea voyages to receive their orders directly on arrival at Pondicherry instead of waiting for months for instructions from Paris.

The tax policy of the Second Empire was significantly altered under the liberal Napoleon III and customs duties on products from the colonies were lowered. In Pondicherry, property taxes were finally lowered and a land register was established. Large-scale irrigation projects were undertaken, especially in Karaikal, in order to increase the yield of rice and millet, restoring some of their vitality to the villages

Opposite page: Pondicherry by Fouqueray, oil on canvas, circa 1930. Réunion des Musées Nationaux.

or *aldeas*. Cash crops such as groundnut and coconut, from which oil was extracted, were developed, although the other crops like indigo and cotton were reduced gradually whilst sugar-cane cultivation almost disappeared.

Industrial activity also started to flourish; oil-mills now used mechanical presses and grinders operated by steam-engines imported from France. After very promising trials at the beginning of the nineteenth century, large spinning-mills were set up. Four important companies were the Rodier Mills, Gaebelé Spinning and Weaving Factory, Kessoram Poddar & Co. and Savana Mills. These mills had the triple advantage of having a large and inexpensive workforce, of motorising mechanical jobs and being able to sell both locally as well as in the international market. However, working conditions were hard, and as in France in the same period, child

Top: The jute factories in the 1930s: Anglo-French Textiles, a well-established modern mill in Pondicherry.
Middle: Transport of indigo. Indigo is a plant used for dyeing, exported since the early 19th century. By the end of the century, trade in indigo had slowly declined.
Bottom: Groundnut harvesting. This commercial crop, which can grow even in poor soil and needs a lot of manpower, was the driving force of Pondicherry's economy in the late 19th century.
Opposite page: Ms Poulain and Duboy's cotton mill in the early 19th century. It was one of the first industrial establishments in India.

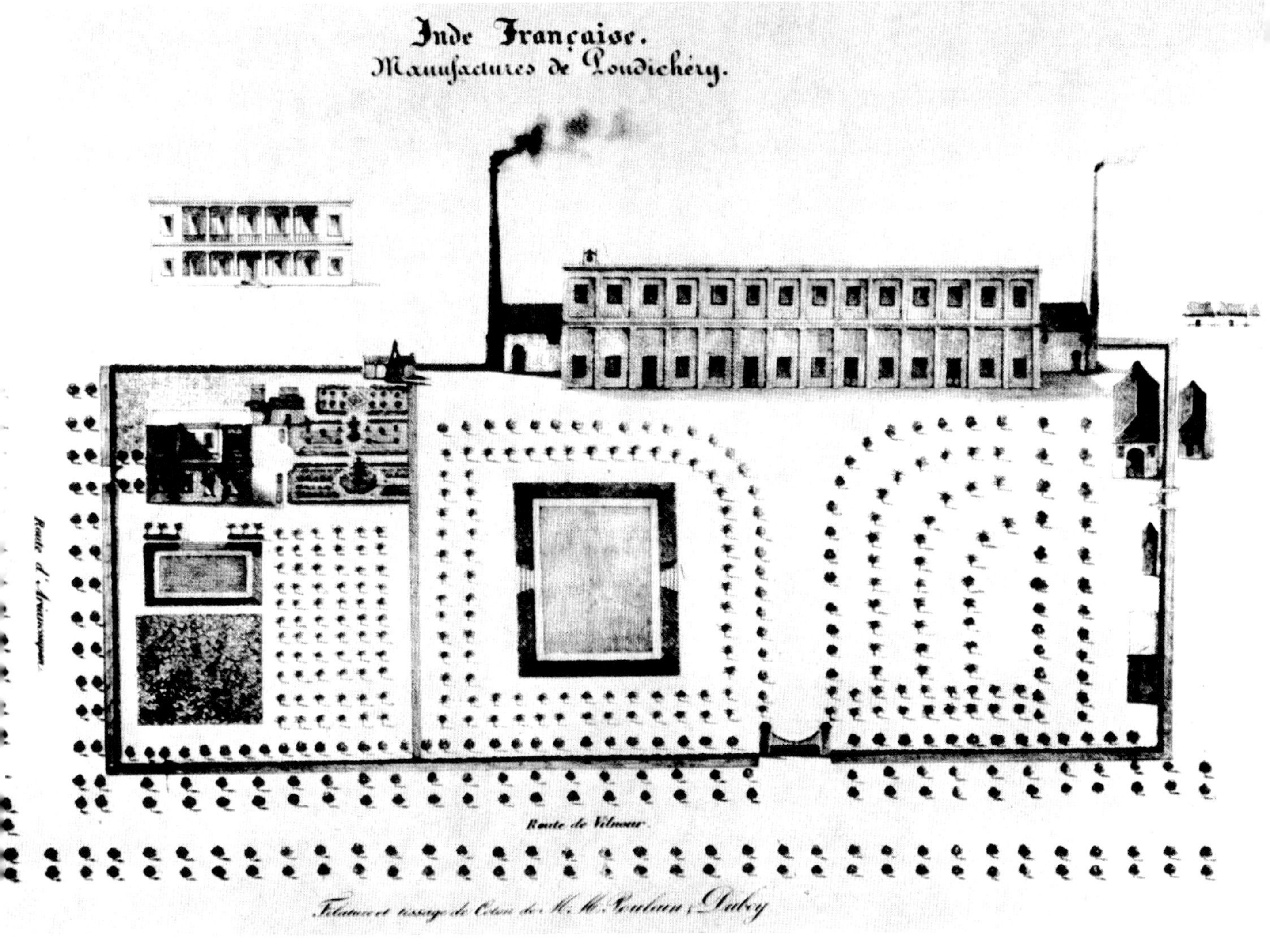
Inde Française.
Manufactures de Pondichéry.
Route de Vilnour.

labour was quite common. Perrotet had already observed back in 1839, the workers suffered from 'unhealthy suffocating dust, which often makes them ill', although he did not mention the extreme heat, which was obviously another serious cross to bear. Either way, apparently nothing much had changed since then.

At the end of the nineteenth century, these factories often belonged to Anglo-French conglomerates, unless they were wholly British. But people in the colony tended to agree with the sharp-witted industrialist Monclar, who observed in 1873: 'The phlegmatic British do not take happily to industry in India. They prefer trade infinitely more... Due to this fact, the French are more comfortable with industry, which in turn has made the British feel duty bound to take up industrial activity in India.'

The commercial activities of Pondicherry, thus, regained some of their former prestige. Internal Indian trade was revived. Exports of Indian textiles increased dramatically. The export of blue cloth, found a ready market among the Touaregs from the cities of Senegal. Small 'cakes' of pressed indigo, and groundnuts, whose cultivation spread rapidly in South India, filled the holds of both French and British steamers. From 1883, Pondicherry became one of the principal exporting ports for groundnuts

in South India. The famous 'Marseilles soap' was made with oil from groundnuts that arrived from Pondicherry. To fuel this spectacular economic growth, the banking system became more organised with the opening of the Indochina Bank in 1875, an important source of investment. It sustained the groundnut trade and financed the construction of imposing warehouses in the south of the town in 1890.

A clientele of captains on long sea voyages, of travel writers such as Pierre Loti, author of *L'Inde sans les Anglais*, stayed at the Hôtel de Paris et de Londres, one of the oldest in Pondicherry. Tourism also developed, right up to Chandernagor, near Calcutta, where the British came to enjoy French liberalism, away from the severe Victorian atmosphere of the capital of British India. Prostitution, licensed by the French authorities, flourished there. In Pondicherry, where the government leased out but regulated the management of distilleries, alcohol and *kallu* flowed freely. In certain years, revenue from this source, it must be admitted, contributed over forty percent of the colony's budget.

Background: View of Pondicherry harbour in the late 19th century. In the foreground, sepoys form part of the 'Greeting Drums' ceremony, welcoming with a volley of cannon shots the ships of the Messageries Maritimes.

French India changed significantly in its appearance: two bridges were constructed on the Gingee river and new roads were laid. In 1866, a landing pier was constructed nearby, to expedite transhipments and do away with the practice of the *chelingues* having to run up onto the beach, always a fearful moment for both passengers and goods. The vestiges of the pier can still be seen out at sea, a few metres from the monument dedicated to Mahatma Gandhi. A fountain was built in 1854 in the centre of the Pondicherry Government Square to distribute a long-awaited system of running water in the 'white' town. The renewal of Pondicherry after 1850 is also reflected in the houses, many of which are from that period. The town regained a certain appeal, offering 'a first impression of grandeur, majesty and serenity', as one of the passengers of a Messageries Maritimes liner observed. 'We looked out of the porthole through which filters the milky light of day and within this copper ring is framed the panorama of Pondicherry: a pier, an iron jetty, forms a spur before a long brownish wharf; above it, all along, square patches of private houses and public buildings, crowned by greyish white balustrades and terraces – the town hall, the shipping services and the harbour office.'

Below: View of Our Lady of the Angels, church in the Saint-Laurent quarter of Pondicherry, in 1863, from the journal *L'Illustration*. Built in 1855 by the engineer Louis Guerre.

Opposite: Our Lady of the Angels church today.

Despite this revitalisation, recovery in Pondicherry remained shaky, due to ceaseless British vigilance, and sometimes even greed: if the British had invested in Pondicherry, it was in part to bypass their own laws. Pondicherry remained under the attentive eye of the British in Madras. On top of this, French India was overtaken by a number of natural catastrophes: the worst drought for a century between 1876 and 1877 and a devastating hurricane in 1885. The *laissez-faire* policy of the Second Empire proved to be an especially double-edged weapon: the extraordinary progress in communications, although it gave French

Opposite: View of Government House in Pondicherry, circa 1860.
Below: Portrait of Louis Guerre, colonial engineer in Pondicherry (1800-1865).

The Opening up of French India and Economic Renewal

Pondicherry in 1891

1. Sepoy barracks
2. Rue des Capucins
3. Chamber of Commerce
4. Government Square
5. The large fountain
6. Government House
7. The residence of the Public Prosecutor
8. The Saint Louis area
9. Square, avenue and statue of Dupleix
10. The Lighthouse
11. Republic Square
12. The flag mast
13. The pier or landing stage
14. The Harbour Office
15. Town Hall
16. Le Cours Chabrol (seafront)
17. Warehouses
18. Rue des Français

India some respite, proved expensive for the Empire when from 1873 onwards, there came a crisis which was to last thirty years and affect both France and her Empire. The arrival of American and British Indian wheat in massive quantities plunged the European economy into a dangerous fall. In 1892, on Jules Méline's initiative, the French Government decided to protect French metropolitan industries by re-imposing customs barriers on colonial products. The British retaliated similarly with the Indian Act of 1895, to protect their Indian market. Then it was revealed that intensive cultivation of groundnuts impoverished the land and caused degeneration of the seed. In 1903, Maurice Maindron, who stayed at the same hotel where Pierre Loti had stayed a few years earlier, wrote: 'The rundown state of L'hôtel de Paris et de Londres is due to the lack of customers. It is not competition, but stagnation in business that has killed it.' For French India, the nineteenth century ended in the doldrums. It would have to wait until the 1920s for a spectacular recovery in its fortunes.

From Illusion to Disillusion

On my way back to Pondicherry in the evening, I saw the statue of Dupleix. He stood in a commanding pose facing the sea, determined, bold, imperious, defiance glinting in his eyes. 'Quite a man,' said an Englishman. 'Gave us a hard time indeed. Of what use is Pondicherry to you at present? You compel us to enforce custom regulations and all our thieves have taken shelter with you! What do you get out of this colony?' 'Nothing at all,' replied a Frenchman, 'but it is important for Dupleix to have his statue in India and to feel at home here.' André Chevrillon, in 1891, could not have expressed the problem better. A colony without colonisers, a colony without any trade worth the name, a colony without prestige. Yet in the late nineteenth century, France held on to French India as to an old family heirloom that one does not want to part with. It is necessary, therefore, to try and understand how France looked upon this little territory which would remain French, at least in title, until 1962.

Opposite page: Frédéric Régamey, Jules Ferry and the representatives of the colony in the French 'Chambre des Députés'. Oil on canvas, 1884. Under the watchful eye of Dupleix, the Empire's future is in discussion, in the conspicuous absence of the representative of French India, Pierre Alype. Château de Versailles, Réunion des Musées Nationaux.

Times of Illusion

The sense of illusion with which the French Third Republic regarded French India and other French colonies was manifestly widespread, but the focus on India was sharper.

A Colony between Two Empires

French India acquired a symbolic role at the end of the nineteenth century, during a period when it seemed trapped between two empires, both literally as well as figuratively – the former, unrealised empire of Dupleix and the new one of Francis Garnier and Savonarole de Brazza in West Africa. In the political discourse of the Third Republic, French India was made to symbolise the colonial destiny of France, to measure up to Great Britain on all the seas of the world and on all the continents, just as France had done in India before, and as it continued to do modestly in late nineteenth century Pondicherry.

Left: Statue of Dupleix in Pondicherry. The colony encouraged and participated in the revival of Dupleix's reputation, one of the oldest French political myths.

Thus from 1870, people started talking about Dupleix once again and about 'the glory of the French in India'. The interest shown in Dupleix during the Second Empire was expressed in new monuments. Dupleix regained his place amongst the great men of France to whom the country was indebted. In 1870, at the request of Governor Bontemps, the Emperor donated a statue of Dupleix to Pondicherry. At the time, it was installed opposite the pier where the statue of Nehru stands today, welcoming passengers of the Messageries Maritimes steamships. Overnight, books were written paying homage to him and newspapers restored him to a place of honour. The greatly romanticised *Dupleix* by Tibulle Haumont became one of the most widely read books by the close of the century. In it, Dupleix appears as a visionary betrayed by the monetary greed of the Compagnie des Indes Orientales and by the negligence of the government of Louis XV. At the end of the century, a Dupleix Committee was formed, headed by a colourful character, the

Right: Portrait of Gabriel Bonvalot in a front page of *Le Monde Illustré* in 1897.

adventurer Gabriel Bonvalot, an archetypal hard-line supporter of the colonial empire. 'It is our duty,' he exhorted, 'to take example from his life and understand how it can help us to build a successful overseas empire.'

In 1897, the bi-centenary of Dupleix's birth, Bonvalot organised one of the strangest ceremonies of the Third Republic in Paris. Poems, songs and plays marked the occasion and Sarah Bernhardt, the greatest actress of the Belle Époque, extolled the great man in this celebration in a new symbolic style.' The newspaper *Le Temps* clearly understood Bonvalot. 'And this is why Gabriel Bonvalot founded the Dupleix Committee' it concluded, 'to give back to the French the taste for colonisation, to open up colonial routes and to provide information, documents and advice.'

This rediscovery of Dupleix occurred alongside French India's entry into an ever-widening French colonial theatre. France, defeated in 1870, was isolated by the diplomacy of Bismarck, first Chancellor of a unified Germany, and thereby prevented from continuing hostilities in Europe. The French nation needed reassuring and focussed on the exploits of pioneering French adventurers abroad for solace. Jean-Baptiste Marchand, who explored Central Africa, and Francis Garnier, who plunged deep into the Indo-China peninsula under the pretext of rescuing the 'White Fathers'. When the Republicans won the elections in 1877, they used colonisation as a means of diverting the attention of the people towards distant horizons where their nationalism and new political experiments could have free play. In 1884, France launched the conquest of Tongking, followed by that of the Indo-China peninsula. Despite setbacks in Indo-China, leading to the resignation of Jules Ferry in 1885, the French advance continued into West Africa with Brazza and Marchand. In the meantime, Britain was also consolidating its territory in East Africa, despite wars in the Transvaal. The rivalry between the imperialist nations led to numerous disputes, giving rise to xenophobia and nationalist sentiments both in England and in France. The most serious of these disputes occurred in 1896 at Fashoda during the British bid to conquer the Sudan, with the aim of creating a chain of colonies from the Mediterranean to the Cape of Good Hope.

Right: Statue of Jeanne d'Arc in Pondicherry. Erected in 1920, it has political significance as it bears witness to the rallying of the Church of France to the Republican regime. In Pondicherry, standing tall alongside British India, she is given the importance of a patron saint.

Thus, in a few years, Dupleix, from being a Bonapartist hero, the original founder of the colonial empire and unrivalled promoter of trade, rose to become a hero of the Republic, a means of denouncing the shortcomings of the monarchy, and of directing the attention of the French public to distant horizons. This French public, however, though ready to applaud French victories, were not prepared to emigrate themselves. Moreover, as the financial scandals in Panama branded the Republicans as opportunists, Dupleix became a focus of extreme anti-British sentiment and hate-filled nationalism, which became an embarrassment to a government which was to sign the Entente Cordiale with Britain in 1904. However, Dupleix remained useful to the group of influential persons, among them eminent journalists, who formed what was called in France the 'Colonial Party'. Their aim was to win over public opinion to induce the French Government to approve new military expeditions, in the name of what they perceived to be the duty of France. Dupleix was chosen as the inspiration of this drive to colonisation between 1870 and 1914. 'France of old, it is affirmed, was ungrateful to Dupleix, but modern France has made amends for the damage done to his fame.'

Below: Chromotype *The Sepoy of India*. The Pondicherry Sepoys were the prototype of the French colonial army.

Opposite: Officers and deputies of the Sepoy company of Pondicherry in 1863 from the journal *L'Illustration*.

Pondicherry, 'the French Dream of India'

In France, between 1870 and 1910, people began to talk again about 'les Établissements français en Inde', the settlements, a trend reflected in the newspapers of the time. Certain clichés of French colonisation re-emerged, revealing a degree of contempt for the subject nations. Most often it was a naïve expression of convictions enunciated by some authority on colonial affairs, like Paul Leroy-Beaulieu or Jules Ferry, coloured by fascination and vague memories of 'the great century'.

The coloniser's image of himself was a recurrent motif in narratives and articles published by the press. It was a commonly-held image, influenced by the theories of a Frenchman, Arthur de Gobineau, which tended to infuse all colonial discourse of the time. It was in fact a warped form of social Darwinism, the theory developed in the 1850s, which saw in humanity diverse races, each corresponding to a different level and potential for progress. Inevitably, the coloniser saw himself at the top of the pyramid. As a textbook of the time explained 'The white race, the most perfect of races, is found mostly in Europe, West Asia, North Africa and America. It is distinguishable by its oval head, a mouth that is not too open and lips that are not too thick.'

The particular mark of France was, nevertheless, its faith in a colonial mission that was quasi-humanist. Colonisation was not about speeches but about deeds, about the determination of Europeans to do good; a duty and a burden, the white man's burden. Literature about the settlements depicted a milieu of peaceful domination. Young civil servants were portrayed under the hypnotic powers of Indian fakirs (religious mendicants) in a town 'where one easily blends with the natives' and where 'the natives are your friends'. The responsibility, the burden of the French civil servant, was to lead this population 'lost in superstition' to French rationality. Essentially, it was conceived as an educational mission. In French colonial discourse, the coloniser was often identified with the schoolteacher. It is from his technique and from his mastery of science that he acquired a near magical power, a view reflected in the newspapers. Thus, in 1870, at the time of the inauguration of the Governor's new building at Karaikal, the editor of *L'Illustration* reiterated that unlike Tamil architecture, the new taste aimed at 'utility'. The positivist, scientific spirit, inspired by the works of Auguste Comte, had

Opposite page: Portrait of a South Indian king around 1910. Heading a small sub-state in the region of Tanjore under British administration, his role had been only honorary for a long time.

already penetrated deeply into the general consciousness. In a short leap, the coloniser, as one who knows how to dispense justice and who has taken upon himself such heavy responsibilities, considers that India is by right his playground and fancies himself as representative of a new aristocracy. In 1879, *Le Journal des Voyages* wrote, 'We met a charming man in Paris, very elegant and highly distinguished, living in the great Indies, who recounted to us after dinner, while smoking an excellent Pino, tales of his tiger-hunting in the plains of Camilla, not far from Chandernagor.'

The coloniser's image of the colonised was also clearly revealed in writings of the period. The Indian is seen to be of inferior rank in the social hierarchy. Though civilised, he still remains backward. He may have some good qualities, like his legendary sweetness of temperament, but he had numerous defects. The insistence of some authors visiting Pondicherry, such as André Chevrillon, on the blackness of the Tamil people, and the pejorative adjectives that he used to describe them, showed that Tamils were considered to be an inferior Indian race with genetic imperfections – an echo of earlier Indology regarding the Aryanisation of South India. Furthermore, the inhabitants of French India were not spared the clichés associated with Asian people in general, the Indian distinguished himself by his predilection for lucre, his wooliness and by the perversity of his traditions. Stories of ritual murders and unimaginable cruelty and tortures abounded. *Sati* was a fashionable theme and the bayaderes or dancers, regarded by many to be mere prostitutes, were also a frequent focus of attention. Even if the white man appeared sure of himself, Hinduism continued to both disturb and fascinate him. André Chevrillon, taking his xenophobia with him to the temples around Pondicherry, wrote in 1891, describing the sculptural figures and bas-reliefs, 'And what comes through in this piling up of deformed figures, with limbs that are twisted and intertwined, is not just irrationality but something savage, perturbing and incomprehensible.' Conversely, the French reassured themselves by pointing in amusement to the splendour of the Rajas who visit Pondicherry, but here, too, the underlying criticism was soon revealed: this display of wealth is merely the hallmark of a useless aristocracy propped up by Britain with the single aim of facilitating its commerce. All these preconceived ideas were naively reported in the press.

However, Paul Leroy-Beaulieu, one of the greatest thinkers of colonial France, considered races to be diverse and set in a hierarchy; he did not assert that individuals

Indian scenes and racial types

Postcards and publicity material between 1890 and 1930. This kind of document was circulated very largely by industrialists and members of the Colonial Party. Pondicherry figures in them quite often and the city's name is associated with many prestigious cultural events.

Below: The Pondicherry *pousse-pousse*. This transport was adopted at the end of the 19th century to replace the palanquin. It was considered more 'humanitarian': the client had full control over his journey.

are completely defined by their race. The colonial task as clearly defined by Jules Ferry, was to bring the subjects of the French Republic to share its values, a process necessarily going beyond any racial differences between coloniser and colonised. The colonialist theories justify exploitation of the raw materials and manpower of the colonies, as the reward for the nation's effort in making France strong

and respected among the great nations, with a combined population of 100 million men and women, a community of which everyone, colonised as well as coloniser, should feel proud. According to these theories, colonisation was a political, economic and philanthropic mission.

Background:
View of the Governement Square, circa 1910-1915.

The Assimilation of French India

'The French colonies are an integral part of the Republic and are subject to the same constitutional laws', declared the Constitution of the Year III of the revolutionary calendar in 1795. Achieving this revolutionary ideal became a political goal for the Republicans of the Third Republic, and French India was chosen to demonstrate the feasibility of the policy to the world.

Assimilation became the official colonial doctrine of the Third Republic from 1876 right up to the years 1895-96. The aim was to lift the colonised to the level of the coloniser. With this in view, the coloniser would progressively confer on the colonised the rights and duties of citizen. This was not in fact a new departure; a precedent had occurred in 1789, when French India sent Representatives to the Assemblée Nationale. Since 1830 the Settlements had had a Council, although its scope was merely advisory and there was only one Indian representative. In 1848, at the proclamation of the Second Republic, it had been decided that the Settlements and the Old Colonies should elect one representative through universal male suffrage to the Metropolitan Chambre des Deputés, but this fell through very soon, partly due to opposition from the French administration in India and the consternation that this announcement caused among the European community.

The broad scope of the Third Republic in 1871 was partly inspired by Victor Schœlcher, abolitionist of slavery and among the most widely recognised authorities on French colonisation. Schœlcher, a committed Republican, was convinced of the universality of the principles guiding France. He argued that cultural progress would only take place when the colonised took charge of their destiny through being given the right to vote as French citizens within the colonial framework. However, his theory rested on the commonly accepted idea that this right should not be exercised everywhere in the same manner and that it should be limited to a select group of colonies which had been related to France for more than 100 years, or which had certain specific characteristics. Schœlcher was, no doubt, thinking of the French West Indies and his incomplete work of abolition there. In light of the Crémieux Decrees of 1871, the followers of Saint Simon wished to begin in Algeria, with the assimilation of the colony's Jews and Spaniards. India, Saint Louis in Senegal and French Cochinchina (Mekong Delta) were equally involved in the project.

French India in colonial exhibitions

Beginning in 1862, colonial exhibitions were regularly organised in France with the aim of developing an interest in the colonies among people in general and business circles in particular.
These were occasions for a curious public, interested in knowledge and commerce, to look at people from an ethnographic viewpoint. They were also opportunities for the colonised people to express their attachment to the French home country.

Right:
The French India pavilion in the 1900 exhibition. Engraving published by *Le Petit Journal*.

Leon Gambetta, influenced by the assimilationists, renewed the proposal of political representation for the Old Colonies and demanded that universal suffrage for men be introduced. Despite total indifference from the majority of Indians, who were probably unaware that an election was being held, Desbassayns de Richemont, a monarchist and son of a previous Governor, was elected Deputy of India.

With the return to power of the Republicans in France in 1877, the political assimilation of the colonies continued steadily and included Pondicherry and the Settlements. In 1880, the General Council was reorganised. In 1881, the legislative elections to the Metropolitan French *Chambre des Députés*, were won by Pierre Alype, a journalist. In the following year, the first seat in the Senate was won by another journalist, Jacques Hébrard. At the same time, local councils were formed and the *Mairie* built in Pondicherry was

soon occupied by a genuine Municipal Council. Elections were held for each of these bodies. To all intents and purposes, it was as if an authentic French *département* had been set up in India. Only the Governor, as direct representative of the French State, continued to be attached to the French army and later to the Minister of Colonies. In India, in addition to the role of a diplomat, he had the same functions as a Metropolitan *préfet*. Thus it was that French India became a model colony – a laboratory, as it has been rightly described, of French colonial theories and Empire. When secular education became mandatory in France during this period, school syllabi required that the names of French India's trading posts be systematically taught, as both the outcome and the springboard of an ongoing campaign.

Above: French officials and Indian civil servants. Picture taken at Pondicherry hospital in the end of the 19th century.

Time of Disillusion

Unfortunately, reality was very different from appearances, and French India came to epitomise the failure of the French colonial project rather than illustrate its success. The first twenty years of universal male suffrage in French India were, in fact, the most dramatic for Republican theory.

The Beginnings of the 'Goonda Raj'

The introduction of universal male suffrage in India was not without repercussions for the colony. In the absence of appropriate preparation, it brought to light major divisions in the French Settlements and resulted in Pondicherry suffering decades of a veritable 'Goonda Raj', a 'government of hooligans'.

An incident in 1873 exposed the weaknesses in the new system. An Indian advocate, Ponnoutamby, entered a courtroom wearing shoes, and thereby became a source of embarrassment to the colonists. He had transgressed the customary law of Mamoul, the traditional Hindu law whose implementation Dupleix had promised to all Indians. Covering the entire gamut of social customs, it laid down the basis of judgement for Indians under the caste system. However, according to the French Napoleonic Code, with its stress on equality under the law, no crime had been committed. The most embarrassing aspect for the colonists – and for Indians of high caste – was that Ponnoutamby appealed under French law and publicly renounced caste customs, thereby placing himself outside Indian society and taking refuge in the arms of France. What is more, he invited Christian Indians, out-castes as well as low castes, to do the same, and in this way founded a party, called by the colonists *Les Renonçants*. Governor Trillard tried to play down this renunciation. 'I doubt, Honourable Minister,' he writes to Paris, 'that there are many Indians who would have recourse to this option – maybe, a few rare Christians who dream only of innovation and assimilation, but as for the pagans, I can declare loudly and clearly that they will be the last to renounce.' The majority, who were primarily Hindu, felt their identity and position, as well as their customs,

Opposite: Scene depicting the election in Allankuppam, a few miles north of Pondicherry, published by *Le Monde Illustré* in 1889. It shows the growing feeling of irritation of the French press against the use of the civic rights by locals.

threatened. The Party of *Les Renonçants*, which at its height numbered no more than 2,000, although it claimed to have 4,500 members, demanded an extension of political rights through a revision of the electoral lists. Until 1880, there were two electoral colleges, one for the Europeans which, in spite of its smaller numbers, carried more weight than the one for the Indians. *Les Renonçants*, who claimed to be Franco-Indian, sought to gain entry into the first electoral college. The Europeans were at a loss, but Paris relished this evident commitment to France. 'French Government policy has always been to try and respect the customs and beliefs of Indians, but never to impose this on them, if they wish to deviate from them.' For the Metropolitan Government, the incident represented the progress of its policy and it approved the change, even though *Les Renonçants* were much smaller in number and sometimes less French-speaking than they claimed to be.

Below: Military review in the late 19th century.

Opposite page: Pondicherry Tribunal. Situated at the location of the present Chief Secretariat, this 18th-century building was the setting for dealing with the political problems.

Top left: Portrait of Angoulevant, Governor of French India in Pondicherry from 1906 to 1908. The Governor strongly supported the 'French idea' of Henri Gaebelé.

Right: Industrialist Henri Gaebelé, leader of the 'French Party' thanks to whom, the 'French idea' which included Republican principles, was revived in Pondicherry after 1906.

Left: Deputy Lemaire. After serving as Governor and opposing the traditionalist Hindus, he managed to get himself elected to the *Chambre des Députés*.

Left: Jules Godin, Senator of India, appointed Minister of Public Works in 1898. *Le Petit Journal* wrote: 'Nothing recommended him for the post that he now occupies, nothing stopped him from accepting it. And so he became Senator of French India.'

The Indians were prepared to use the weapons that France had given them with admirable skill, and not only in one direction. Chanemougam, a prominent citizen described by supporters as 'deeply religious, almost mystic', a man endowed with remarkable intelligence, sought to impede the assimilationists. First, he took advantage of the two elections with universal suffrage, the legislative and the senatorial. It is he who struck a deal with the French journalists who announced their candidature in the national elections. Pierre Alype was at that time editing *Le Journal des Colonies*, a small newspaper, and Jacques Hébrard's brother was the editor of *Le Temps*, the Third Republic's most influential newspaper. They had the mission of defending, by hook or by crook, the ideas of Nadou Chanemougam. As for the elections, they were mere formalities; they were rigged in advance and thanks to generous libations of *kallu*, the local coconut alcohol, the turnout of voters rose swiftly. Alype remained a deputy for over sixteen years and Chanemougam made use

Below: Pondicherry Law College, built at the end of the 1870s.

of his influence to undermine the hopes of *Les Renonçants* in Paris.

Although this did not happen without some resistance, French India gradually disintegrated into a country of electoral scandals, a process which continued right up to the Second World War. In 1884, an important and heated exchange took place in the press concerning the Right to Renunciation and the need to settle it once and for all. Victor Schœlcher himself was the author of a decree which divided the electoral body into three colleges, which was hardly satisfactory to anyone. Chanemougam continued his campaign, increasing his electoral majority by the same methods. The political atmosphere became ever more oppressive, and elections turned into nightmares. Each party, and indeed the administration itself, was prepared to use the most violent means to

Below: Postcard, circa 1900. Coumetis Street adjoins Chettys Street. The roads are not paved, but treated with *caliman*, crushed brick mixed with mud. On either side, a network of side-streets, is laid out (*thalvaram* and *thinnai*). On the left can be seen Calve Supraya Chettyar's house with its upper storey.

The 'black' town and its prominent citizens, the notables

Up to the 1920s, the focus of the French authorities was the 'white' town; the 'black' town saw hardly any improvements in sanitation. For the most part it was left to prominent Indians to beautify it and fit it out with the necessary infrastructure. In this way, they expressed their religious commitment and cultivated their influence by donations and charity work. At the end of the nineteenth century, among the most renowned was Calve Supraya Chettyar, who endowed a choultry and a school, '*un collège*', and maintained several temples.

achieve its ends. Finally in 1893, the colony crumbled under the weight of serious riots which, when reported in France, sounded the death knell of the doctrine of political assimilation. In 1906 the *Journal des Débats* wrote: 'Universal suffrage in India is a tumour that resists all remedies. There is but one surgery which can be effective – pure and simple elimination of the right to vote, consenting to which has been a terrible mistake.' Colonial representation from India, the West Indies, Africa and Cochinchina, was rejected wholesale. Instead many people supported the idea of association, or the idea of fundamentally separate ways of development, and with it the complete suspension of democratic institutions in the colonies.

In fact, such a change of policy did not take place, but the French Government, it is true, did not pursue the establishment of any more assimilated colonies until the attempt to save the Empire with the French Union in 1946. Within the colony the status quo was maintained, mostly because the French oligarchy in Pondicherry, led by the industrialist Henri Gæbelé, managed to regain control over most of the political institutions between 1906 and 1914. He was Chairman of the Chamber of Commerce, Mayor of the city, Chairman of the Local Assembly and finally Senator of French India. His allies had total control of the port and the boatmen of Pondicherry were used as the new shock troops of the French party. Around 1918, the last political adversaries openly talked about his nepotism. They were weak no doubt but not yet disarmed. They raised their head again in the 1920s: a Franco-Hindu party bringing together those most hostile to legal assimilation, continued to demand one common electoral list and finally succeeded in dethroning the old leader in the 1928 elections.

An evaluation of this first 'Goonda Raj', however negative it might have been for Republican institutions in French India, does indicate, nevertheless, some progress and change in the nature of political debate. The question at issue in Chanemougam's struggle had been the pre-eminence of Indians over Europeans and *Les Renonçants*. At a later stage, each group divided further in a process which offered new opportunities for compromise, alliance and agreement, thereby making the political scene infinitely richer, although unfortunately no less brutal, during elections.

Opposite page: Gathering of French expatriates at the Cercle de Pondichéry. Circa 1890.

Pondicherry and Indian Nationalism

Curiously, although it might seem much attached to France, French India would become what English authorities have called, not always unfairly, 'a nest of Indian nationalists'. Between 1890 and 1910, the first seeds of Indian nationalism sprouted in Bengal, triggered by the British decision to partition Bengal. Inspired by the Irish struggle against the British crown, revolutionary groups formed in Calcutta, recruiting young men who were often well-educated and from good families. These groups, many of whom loosely recognised Sri Aurobindo's inspiring political leadership, entered the fray by organising bomb attacks targeted at British officers and authorities in 1907.

Training and preparation for these attacks took place in hidden backyards, and when the British police started to tighten the security net, the insurgents took shelter in nearby Chandernagor under the protection of French sovereignty. The French authorities were regularly informed by the English about the presence of these 'terrorists' as there were a significant number of spies on their payroll within the Settlement. The French were quite aware of the situation but the British considered the French response altogether too feeble and decided to initiate action themselves, even if it involved violating French sovereignty.

French reaction was swift and the British ambassador was asked for explanations. Incidents of this kind happened regularly up until the 1920s. It was in Pondicherry that Sri Aurobindo decided to take shelter in 1910, to the great displeasure of the British who immediately demanded his extradition. This was refused by Henri Gæbelé, the town Mayor and Senator, even though the Governor seemed willing to respond to the British demands. Sri Aurobindo had been preceded by other Indian revolutionaries and nationalists, such as Calve Sankara Chettyar and Aiyar, as well as the poet Subramanian Bharati, who was an active member of Congress and who, thanks

Left: Sri Aurobindo, circa 1918. After his withdrawal from active politics in 1910, he became a symbol of spiritual and moral strength for the independence movement.

to his stay in Pondicherry, had embraced Republican ideals.

To understand this situation, it is important to remember that the French administration had little real control over the activities of their Indian fellow-citizens. This partly explains their weak response to British demands. However, there was also a degree of sympathy for the nationalists, who were often well-educated and able to speak several European languages. 'He reads Greek and Latin!' exclaimed with great stupefaction the examining magistrate who was asked to issue a search warrant against Sri Aurobindo in 1912. There remained too, a lingering defiance towards Britain, combined with a strong sense of national pride, even at a time when the Franco-British alliance was at its most cordial. Events and attitudes in Paris were far removed from India.

It was a strongly held belief that citizens of French India were unlikely to be tempted by calls for independence. Many distinguished Indians had no wish to change administrations. They led a good life under these laws, perhaps even better than if the colony were to become independent. Both Indians and Europeans were able to enjoy the advantages offered by French India when the port of Pondicherry unexpectedly took on a new lease of life. Meanwhile *Les Renonçants* remained quietly in the background.

Above: The poet Bharathi, picture circa 1910.IFP-EFEO.

Opposite page:
Sri Aurobindo Ashram
in the early 1950s.
Founded by Mira Alfassa,
the Mother, in 1926,
the Ashram was not
the hotbed of political agitation
which the British liked to believe.
It was a place to try out
other paths that could lead
to independence
(picture by M. Vidyavrata).

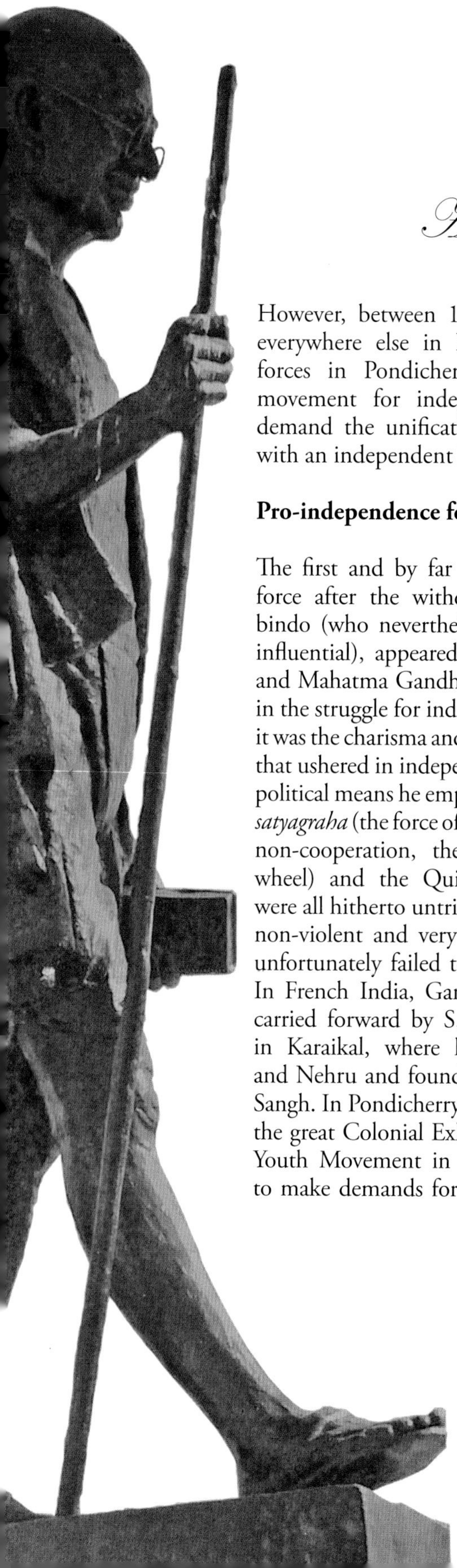

A March towards Independence

However, between 1914 and 1946, like everywhere else in India, a number of forces in Pondicherry would join the movement for independence and later demand the unification of French India with an independent India.

Pro-independence forces

The first and by far the most important force after the withdrawal of Sri Aurobindo (who nevertheless continued to be influential), appeared when the Congress and Mahatma Gandhi assumed leadership in the struggle for independence. Certainly it was the charisma and influence of Gandhi that ushered in independence in India. The political means he employed, in the form of *satyagraha* (the force of truth), political fasts, non-cooperation, the *chakhra* (spinning wheel) and the Quit India Movement, were all hitherto untried political methods, non-violent and very effective but which unfortunately failed to stave off partition. In French India, Gandhi's campaign was carried forward by S. Rangasamy Naiker in Karaikal, where he received Gandhi and Nehru and founded the Harijan Seva Sangh. In Pondicherry, in 1931, the year of the great Colonial Exhibition in Paris, the Youth Movement in French India began to make demands for social reform and a single unified electoral list. When Gandhi visited Pondicherry on 17th February 1934, he stressed the need for fraternity between the different communities of India.

The second force pushing for independence was the social movement. It was very important, especially in South India and in the big industrial cities, for two reasons: firstly, the economic crisis of the 1930s affected both British and French India, leading to unemployment and a slowing down and gradual decline of trade; secondly the local European spinning mills employed a significant number of semi-qualified, barely educated and low-paid employees who were encouraged by the presence of several freedom fighters and by communists to organise clandestine unions. French social law on trade unionism was not fully operational in India even though it had been recognised since the 1884 Waldeck–Rousseau law in France. In 1936, the year of the *Front Populaire* in France, strikes broke out in the Savana Mills, where the director was locked up. The Governor ordered the sepoys to open fire and at least twelve people were killed. For many, this revealed the true face of the colonial system: 'The slightest demands for a rise in salary are met grudgingly and guns gag all protests,' explained Bernard Pounnou Delafon in 1945.

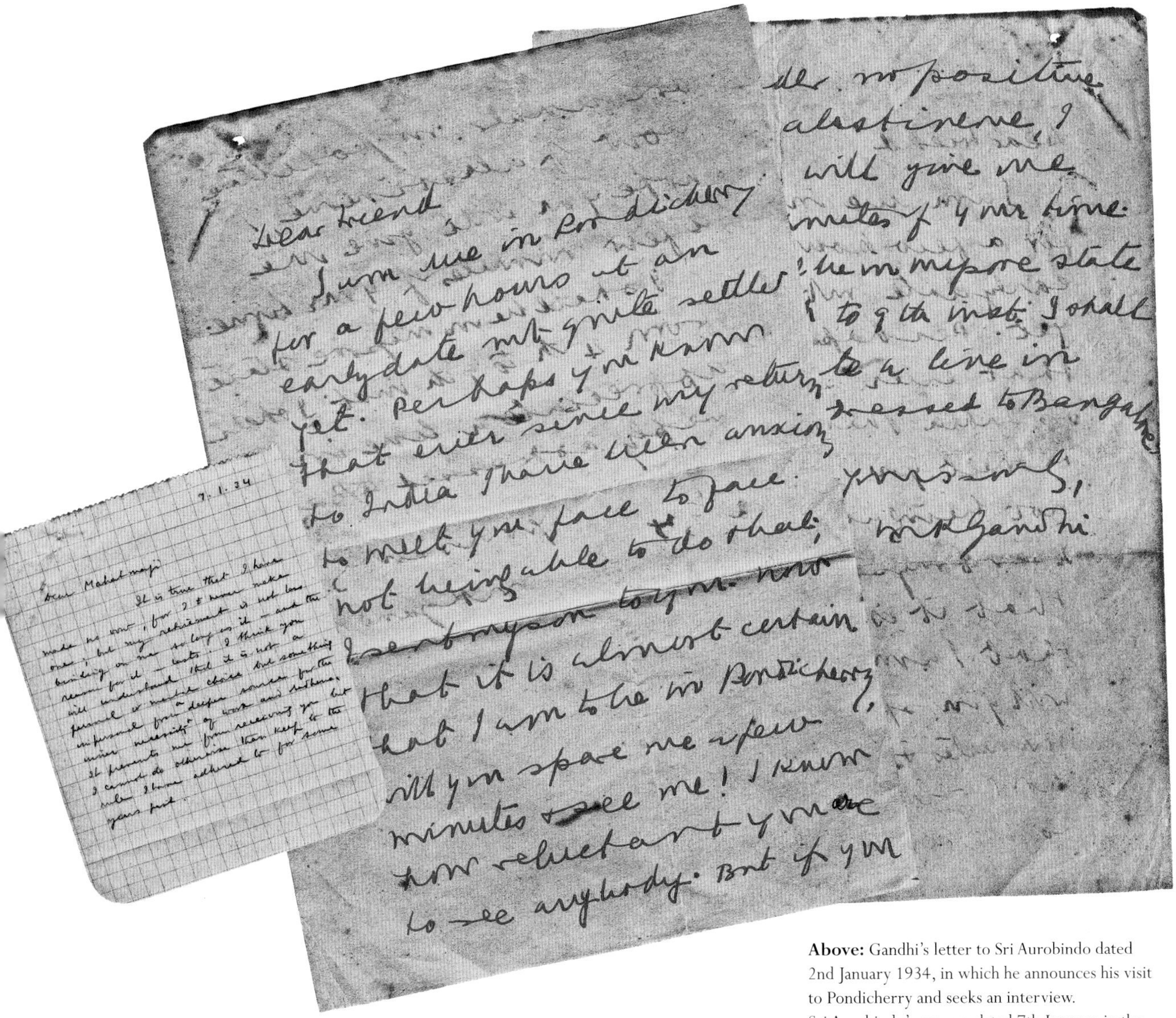
Dear Friend
I am due in Pondichery
for a few hours at an
early date not quite settled
yet. Perhaps you know
that ever since my return
to India I have been anxious
to meet you face to face.
not being able to do that,
I sent my son to you. Now
that it is almost certain
that I am to be in Pondicherry,
will you spare me a few
minutes & see me! I know
how reluctant you are
to see anybody. But if you

…der no positive
abstinence, I
will give me
…minutes of your time.
…be in Mysore state
…to 9th inst. I shall
…a line in
…essed to Bangalore.
Yours sincerely,
M K Gandhi

7. 1. 34
Dear Mahatmaji
It is true that I have
made no vow, for I never make
one, but my retirement is not less
binding on me so long as it – and the
reason for it – lasts. I think you
will understand that it is not a
personal or mental choice but something
impersonal from a deeper source for the
inner necessity of work and sadhana.
It prevents me from receiving you but
I cannot do otherwise than keep to the
rule I have adhered to for some
years past.

Above: Gandhi's letter to Sri Aurobindo dated 2nd January 1934, in which he announces his visit to Pondicherry and seeks an interview. Sri Aurobindo's answer, dated 7th January, in the hand of his secretary, reiterates the impossibility of his coming out of his retreat.

The social movement in Pondicherry, as elsewhere, was controlled by the Communist Party. It was an Indian national, Manabendra Roy, who defined the communist stance vis-à-vis the colonies and founded the underground Communist Party of India. He had been a member of Bengali terrorist groups in his youth. The Communist International decided to support an Indian revolution and, after several rounds of discussion from 1923 onwards, lent its support also to the 'traditionalist' independence movements. In French India, it was Roy's line of thought that prevailed, as it was applicable to all colonised countries. The first political communist leader in Pondicherry was Subbiah who came from the French Communist Party and who led a regrouping of the parties fighting for independence and social justice, known as the National Democratic Front after 1945. Although elected senator, he was forced to go underground in 1948 after openly demanding independence for the Indian Settlements as well as for Indo-China.

Opposite page: View of the pier of Pondicherry in the late 1940s by M. Vidyavrata. Boatmen, though very attached to tradition, were the first group of workers acting as a union in Pondicherry.

Conservative forces

Conservative forces were also numerous in French India: both town-dwellers and villagers remained untouched by the culture of the colonisers. Most of them were largely indifferent to the political issues at stake and, unfortunately, at the time of elections, would fall prey to the 'batonists' (a form of 'political press gangs'), who would wield batons and drag them to the ballot office to vote for their employers. However, within a few short years, the pro-Gandhi supporters and the Communists had succeeded in promoting greater political awareness.

The Europeans and the descendants of Europeans were naturally attached to France. Most of them did not see any reason to change their lifestyle. Most of them supported De Gaulle because they saw him as defender of the Empire. After the war, a large number of them decided to remake their lives in France.

Top: Governor Bonvin's arrival on the Messageries Maritimes ship *Le Phoenix*, receiving warm welcome from the *chelingues* of the Pondicherry Port.

Middle: Governor Bonvin inspecting troops on his arrival in front of Pondicherry's massed population.

Bottom: Pondicherry Red Cross Committee, chaired by Mrs Bonvin, in support of the war effort.

French India at war

Right: Publication of the Government of French India, 1942.

Below: Arrival of Sir Arthur Oswald Hope, Governor of Madras, at Government House in December 1942.

L'INDE FRANÇAISE DANS LA GUERRE

«Ce sont les «ÉTABLISSEMENTS FRANÇAIS DE L'INDE», les minuscules possessions que la France a gardées du temps où elle avait toutes les Indes, qui se sont ralliées les premières à la France Libre.

Les vieux ports fameux de Pondichéry, de Chandernagor, de Mahé, de Karikal ont informé le Général qu'ils refusaient l'armistice et qu'ils continuaient la guerre aux côtés des Français Libres et des Anglais.»

(CHARLES DE GAULLE)
par Philippe Barrès

Left: Protocol dinner during the visit of Sir Arthur Oswald Hope, Governor of Madras, in December 1942.

A March towards Independence

Among the minority party of *Les Renonçants* the attachment to France was almost as strong. Although under pressure from their compatriots, many among them took up arms for De Gaulle during the Second World War, following the example of their parents, who in many cases had fought and died at Verdun.

Then, too, many prominent Indians and Creoles were very ambivalent with regard to the pro-independence groups. They knew that they had the upper hand in French India and could live comfortably under traditional Indian customs which turned a blind eye to certain contraband activities. They were especially wary of the young, socialist reformers of Congress, including Nehru. For them, an independent India could eventually lead to a more restrictive India.

However, the principal force of conservatism continued to be the Government in Paris. By 1946, Premier Leon Blum was quite aware of the inevitability of Indian independence. Maurice Schumann, one of the founders of modern Europe, was sent to Pondicherry to propose the setting up of a Franco-

Opposite page: View of the War Memorial for the Dead, by M. Vidyavrata. Constructed in 1937, it was an expression of gratitude as well as a symbol of France's attachment to its Old Colonies.

Indian university to preserve French cultural influence. However, the outbreak of hostilities in Indo-China in 1947 gave the Settlements a renewed strategic importance. For a large majority on the political right, giving up the Settlements would open the door to decolonisation of the whole Empire; it was out of the question. In 1945, at Setif in Algeria, government policy had already led to the killing of a significant number of civilians. So it was that French India became a part of the French Union as part of a last ditch effort to play for time and to honour promises made during the war, It was this combination of assimilationist and associative doctrines which brought the colony considerable autonomy, with the creation of a French Indian Representative Assembly and with the Governor being nominated Commissioner of the Republic.

Below: Photograph of the 'Comité des non-castés' in 1945. It was one of the pro-French organisations uniting Indians and Europeans.

Confrontation

With the advent of independence in British India in 1947, conflict became unavoidable. As French India moved towards independence, it became clear that the matter had repercussions far beyond this small colony. From 1946 to 1954, tensions increased. In 1947, Gandhi himself had to intervene to restore peace: 'France is a big country and a friend of liberty. India should not give France reason to worry.' France declared that it was ready to leave but only after a referendum. This thinly veiled ploy to use a referendum to retain power in Pondicherry fooled nobody and after 1949, independent India flatly opposed this procedure. The situation remained blocked until Mendès-France came to power in France on 19th June 1954.

Hostilities between the two nations could no longer be avoided. Becoming impatient, Nehru established a customs barrier around the colony, thereby comp-

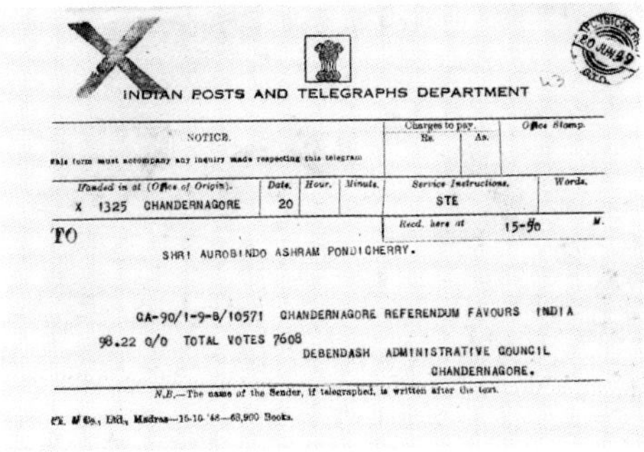

INDIAN POSTS AND TELEGRAPHS DEPARTMENT

20 JUN 49

NOTICE. This form must accompany any inquiry made respecting this telegram	Charges to pay. Rs.	As.	Office Stamp.

Handed in at (Office of Origin).	Date.	Hour.	Minute.	Service Instructions.	Words.
X 1325 CHANDERNAGORE	20			STE	

Recd. here at 15-50 M.

TO

SHRI AUROBINDO ASHRAM PONDICHERRY.

GA-90/1-9-B/10571 CHANDERNAGORE REFERENDUM FAVOURS INDIA 98.22 o/o TOTAL VOTES 7608

DEBENDASH ADMINISTRATIVE COUNCIL CHANDERNAGORE.

N.B.—The name of the Sender, if telegraphed, is written after the text.

Top: Joseph David in 1942. He effectively controlled the colony from the late 1930s.

Middle: Telegram announcing the Chandernagor election results to Sri Aurobindo in 1949.

Bottom: Old pier damaged by the November 1952 cyclon. Many saw that event as a sign of the French rule at its end.(Pic. EFEO-IFP.)

letely isolating Pondicherry and stopping any profitable smuggling trade with the subcontinent. Barbed wire fences were erected and machine-guns placed in position. In the event of a major crisis, the French made plans to bring in supplies to Pondicherry by sea. To further intimidate the other trading posts, India supported armed liberation groups from neighbouring states. The message for France was clear. It was time for them to leave, just as the British had done, and the Portuguese would be forced to do. Behind the scenes, diplomatic channels were explored and V.K. Krishna Menon became one of the principal instruments in the reunification of Pondicherry with independent India. On the fringes of the 1954 Geneva conference, he worked to convince Pierre Mendès-France, even though the decision seemed to have already been taken by Paris. Pressure from independent India accentuated the differences between the various trading posts. In 1949, India obtained a resounding success by agreeing to a referendum in Chandernagor. Close to Calcutta and geographically more continental than the other Settlements, Chandernagor, which had

Opposite page: Changing of the Guard in front of the Governor's Palace, in the late 1940s (photo by M. Vidyavrata).

been largely ignored by both Pondicherry and Paris, came out with a ninety-eight percent 'yes' vote for unification with India. In 1954 India took over unilateral control in Yanam and Mahe without encountering any serious opposition. Opinion in Pondicherry was sharply divided. The Indian archives have preserved a record of Jawaharlal Nehru's interview with the French Governor Baron in 1947: 'There were two underlying reasons for the dilemma in Pondicherry: the first was its attachment to India as a Motherland, the second, was its attachment to France due to hundreds of years of union with France and French culture.' In 1954, at a time when the government of Pierre Mendès-France seemed ready to settle the question without recourse to a referendum, for fear of not receiving a massive vote for France, Goubert, pillar of the French presence, and leader of the Socialist Party and its numerous 'batonists', switched sides and declared himself in favour of independence, thereby much reducing the risk of disturbances and a rigged referendum. Whether this change of loyalty was triggered by a sense of geopolitical realism, by nationalist conviction or even well thought-out personal interest, we shall probably never know.

As a result, Administrator André Ménard took fright and approached Captain Arnold, Chief Inspector of the Messageries Maritimes, who happened to be on tour in Pondicherry, about re-routing one of the steamships on the Indo-China line for a possible evacuation. In a report to the Director of the Messageries Maritimes about his visit on 10 June 1954

Left: Award of medals in the 1950s. To receive a medal was the greatest honour that one could get in Pondicherry.

Oppposite page: A '*Macoua*' of the Corommandel coast in Pondicherry, circa 1950.

Captain Arnold wrote: 'I replied to the Governor that we were at the service of the nation and that we would naturally take responsibility for such a mission. I assured him that you would, if necessary divert the required ships to Pondicherry and that one of our big Far East steamships was already on its way.' A few days later, André Ménard was sent police reinforcements, which provoked immediate complaint from New Delhi. Monseigneur Colas, archbishop of Pondicherry, brought a note of to common sense to the debate: 'It is far better to leave with a smile, gaining some advantages for French influence, than to leave with a kick on the...' The decision to proceed with the Merger, a re-reunification of Pondicherry with India, was discreetly passed to avoid any further outside interference. In an assembly meeting at Kilianur, a village far removed from all agitation, the vote to join India was taken in October 1954. On 1st November, power was transferred to the Government of India. The twilight of the Settlements was to last eight years, the transitional period guaranteed under the treaty for sorting out interests in the former colony. De facto transfer of control had already occurred, but the territories belonged de jure to France up to 16th August 1962. For many the attachment to France was deep and the transition caused profound unease. Some Pondicherrians, French citizens by right, realised that Indian nationality would not guarantee happiness. Others who felt emotionally closer to India, experienced another kind of painful dilemma.

The treaty guaranteed their continued French nationality, on presentation of a

pile of official documents, not readily or easily available in those days. With the date of the definitive transfer approaching, and after a period of dithering inaction, many hurried to the French Consulate to register themselves as best as they could with the smattering of French at their command. On 16th August 1962, the definitive transfer day, the queue in front of the Consulate was so long that everybody was ushered inside and the registration process continued through the night, even if that meant pre-dating the documents by a few hours. An overwhelming majority of the population, however, became Indian citizens and participated in the development of Pondicherry as a Territory of the Indian Union.

The last days of the French in India

From 1949 to 1954, Pondicherry was suspended in an end-of-reign atmosphere of part indifference and part anguish, overtaken by the unfolding events.

Opposite: The Republic's Administrator, André Ménard (foreground) at the Villianur temple festival, circa 1953.

Centre: The archbishop of Pondicherry, Monseigneur Colas, in the early 1940s.

Bottom: Signing of the de facto treaty of cession at Government House between Kewal Singh and Mr Landy, 1st November 1954.

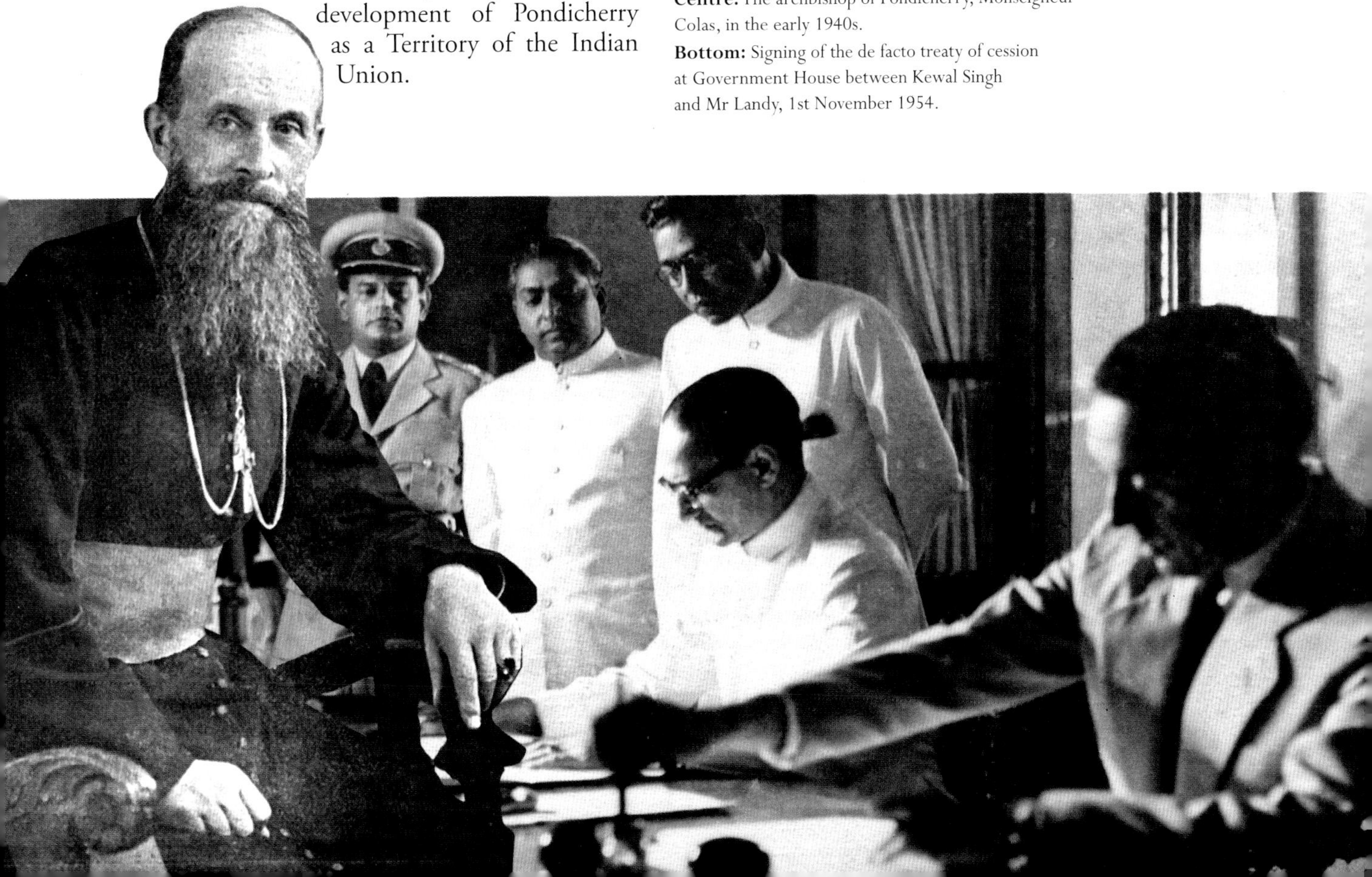

Pondicherry Today...

Fifty years later, the last vestiges of the colonial past are gradually disappearing, although not forgotten. The long journey was never easy or straightforward, and memories of Pondicherry's colonial history may sometimes be painful, but it is from this past that the future will be constructed.

Over the years, the town has changed a lot. The population has grown exponentially, due especially to migration from the surrounding countryside which has led to an unresolved housing shortage. During the 1980s and 1990s, some fifty suburbs or *nagars*, were developed. In a phenomenon not unknown to European cities, the economic boom of the 1990s heralded the arrival of real estate speculation, which pushed up real estate prices and incited house-owners to pull down old buildings. In 2006, the Indian press claimed an 8.1 per cent economic growth rate in India. The nation has become significantly richer and the middle classes are looking for comforts that traditional houses can no longer provide. On the other hand, in times of great change, people need roots and seek a sense of continuity which will always find expression.

Today the Union Territory of Pondicherry is proud of its uniqueness in India. The French art of living, the *pétanque* players, the old houses, whether colonial or Tamil, are all signs that, at least for Indians, Nehru's French window on India has remained open. If the trilingualism of Tamil, French and English envisaged by the Treaty of Cession has not been quite realised, the Sri Aurobindo Ashram, the 'heart of the city' as Governor Baron considered it, is a living seat of the French language. *Les Optants* or those who chose French citizenship in 1962, continue to interact with the country and return every summer, bringing back a whiff of France in their bags and lifestyle that lingers on long after they disappear again. Some French civil servants were able to stay on as the Cession Treaty allowed France to maintain several institutions: a Consulate, a *Lycée Français* or high school, the *Institut Français de Pondichéry* and the *École Française d'Extrême-Orient*.

Pondicherry can rightfully boast of its many advantages: a cosmopolitan and open population, excellent hospitals, a growing university, an invaluable French library, an attractive urban setting, well worth restoring and protecting and an Ashram renowned both in India and abroad. The ability to navigate periods of transition could open Pondicherry to a unique destiny as the intellectual, cultural and service sector capital of South India.

Opposite page: A house in Pondicherry in the 'black' town. The architectural Indian heritage is threatened most here. The walls of many houses belonging to the notables from the French period are in a bad state as the families gradually became poorer. Today, vast sums of money are being offered to them to sell their family property and vacate it. A good number of buildings in the 'black' town have already been pulled down to give way to apartment blocks or shopping complexes, which are financially much more profitable for the real-estate developers. The rare old buildings that still stand today have often been under litigation, sometimes for several decades. The absence of legislation to protect heritage casts a menacing shadow on the avowed policy of developing Pondicherry as a tourist destination.

Below: Houses 8 and 9 in Rue de la Marine. The houses in the 'white' town are, relatively, in a better state of conservation, even though beautiful edifices keep disappearing regularly. The house-owners here are more attached to their family heritage. The Sri Aurobindo Ashram has kept a large number of buildings in a good state. Ambitious restoration work is being carried out by the local government and different associations for the protection of the local heritage.

Bibliography

On India:

Danielou, Alain, *Histoire de l'Inde,* Paris: Fayard, 1971.

Jaffrelot, Christophe, dir., *L'Inde contemporaine de 1950 à nos jours*, Paris: Fayard, 1997.

Lombard, Denys, dir., *Rêver l'Asie – Exotisme et littérature coloniale aux Indes, Indochine et Insulinde*, Paris: EHESS, 1993.

Markovits, Claude, dir., *Histoire de l'Inde moderne, 1480-1950*, Paris: Fayard, 1994.

Weinberger-Thomas, Catherine, *L'Inde et l'imaginaire*, Paris: EHESS, 1988.

Meyer, Eric, *Une histoire de l'Inde – Les Indiens face à leur passé,* Paris: Albin Michel, 2007.

On foreign trade in India:

Devèze, Michel, *L'Europe et le monde à la fin du xviii*^{e} *siècle*, Paris: Albin Michel, 1970.

Guillaume, Pierre, *Le monde colonial, xix*^{e}*-xx*^{e} *siècle*, Paris: Armand Colin, 1974.

Haudrère, Philippe, *La Compagnie française des Indes au xviii*^{e} *siècle (1719-1795)*, Paris: Les Indes Savantes, 2005.

Haudrère, Philippe, *Les Compagnies des Indes Orientales – Trois siècles de rencontre entre Orientaux et Occidentaux*, Paris: Desjonquières, 2006.

Haudrère, Philippe, Le Bouëdec, Gérard, *Les Compagnies des Indes*, Rennes: Ouest-France, 1999.

Morineau, Michel, *Les Grandes Compagnies des Indes Orientales*, (xvie-xixe siècles), Paris: PUF, 1994.

Villiers, Patrick, Duteil, *L'Europe, la mer et les colonies, xvii*^{e}*-xviii*^{e} *siècle*, Paris: Hachette, 1997.

On French colonization:

Blanchard, Blanchoin, Bancel, Boëych, Gerbeau, *L'autre et nous, « scènes et types »*, Paris: Syros-Achac, 1995.

Binoche Guèdra, Jacques, *La France d'Outre mer (1815-1962)*, Paris: Masson, 1992.

Girardet, Raoul, *L'idée coloniale en France*, Paris: Table ronde, 1972.

Meyer, Tarrade, Rey Goldzeiguer, Thobie, *Histoire de la France coloniale*, Tome 1, *Des origines à 1914*, Paris: Armand Colin, 1990.

Thobie, Meynier, Coquery-Vidrovitch, Ageron, *Histoire de la France coloniale*, Tome 2, *1914-1990*, Paris: Arnand Colin, 1991.

Schmidt, Nelly, *Victor Schœlcher*, Paris: Fayard, 1993.

On Pondicherry and the French presence in India:

Anthony, Francis Cyril, *The Gazetteer of India*, U. T. of Pondicherry, Pondicherry, Administration of the Union Territory, 1982.

Annousamy, David, *L'intermède français en Inde – Secousses politiques et mutations juridiques,* Paris: L'Harmattan, 2005.

David, Georgette, *Pondichéry, porte de l'Inde*, Pondicherry: All India Press, 1995.

David, Georgette, *Pondichéry, des comptoirs français à l'Inde d'aujourd'hui*, Pondicherry: Kaïlash, 2004.

INTACH, *Architectural Heritage of Pondicherry – Tamil and French Precincts*, Pondicherry: Intach, 2004.

Mathews, K.S., *The French in India and Indian Nationalism (1700-1963)*, New Delhi: B.R.Publishing Corp., 1999.

Ramassamy, A., *History of Pondicherry*, New-Delhi: Sterling Publishers, 1987.

Vincent, Rose, *L'aventure des Français en Inde, xviie-xxe siècles*, Coll. Asie imaginaire histoire, Pondicherry: Kaïlash, 1998.

Weber, Jacques, *Compagnies et comptoirs – L'Inde des Français, xviiie-xixe siècles*, Paris: Société Française d'Histoire d'Outre-mer, 1991.

Weber, Jacques, *Les relations entre la France et l'Inde de 1673 à nos jours*, Paris: Les Indes savantes, 2002.

Right: Young Hindu girl, lithograph, early 19th century.

On the 17th and 18th centuries:

Bourdat, Pierre, *Pondichéry xviiie siècle*, Pondicherry: All India Press, 1993.

Lafont, Jean-Marie, *Chitra, Cities and Monuments of Eighteenth-century India from French Archives*, New Delhi: Oxford University Press, 2001.

Deleury, Guy, *Le voyage en Inde – Anthologie des voyageurs français*, 1750-1820, Paris: Robert Lafont, Coll. Bouquins, 1991.

Deloche, Jean, *Le papier terrier de la ville blanche de Pondichéry, 1777*, Pondicherry: IFP-EFEO, 2002.

Deloche, Jean, *Origin of the Urban Development of Pondicherry according to the Seventeenth Century Dutch Plans*, Pondicherry: IFP-EFEO, 2004.

Deloche, Jean, *Le vieux Pondichéry (1673-1824) – Revisité d'après les plans anciens*, Pondicherry: IFP-EFEO, 2005.

Labernadie, Marguerite, *Le vieux Pondichéry*, Paris, 1936.

Haudrère, Philippe, *Les Français dans l'Océan Indien au xviiie siècle – La Bourdonnais et Rostaing*, Paris: Les Indes Savantes, 2005.

Vigié, Marc, *Dupleix*, Paris: Fayard, 1993.

Vincent, Rose, *Pondichéry, 1674-1761 – L'échec d'un rêve d'empire*, Paris: Autrement, 1993.

Sen, S.P., *The French in India, 1763-1816*, Calcutta, 1958.

On the 19th and 20th centuries:

Weber, Jacques, *Pondichéry et les comptoirs des Indes après Dupleix – La démocratie au pays des castes*, Paris: Denoël, 1996.

Weber, Jacques, *Les Établissements français de l'Inde au xixe siècle (1816-1914)*, Paris: Librairie de l'Inde, 1988.

Govindin, Sulfy Santa, *Les Engagés indiens – Île de la Réunion, xixe siècle*, Saint-Denis: Azalées, 1994.

On decolonization:

Heehs, Peter, *The Bomb in Bengal – The Rise of Revolutionary Terrorism in India, 1900-1910*, New Delhi, Oxford University Press, 1993.

Arpi, Claude, *La politique française de Nehru – la fin des comptoirs français de l'Inde (1947-1954)*, Auroville, Pavillon de France, 2002.

Collectif, *Il y a cinquante ans... Pondichéry – L'intégration des établissements français en Inde*. Perspectives historiques et culturelles, Auroville, Auroville Press, 2004.

Neogy, S., *Indian Nationalism and French Decolonisation*, Pondicherry, IFP, 2005.

Right: Brahmin schoolmaster, lithograph, early 19th century.

Acknowledgements

The author would like to warmly thank here all the individuals and institutions who have directly and indirectly contributed to the publication of this illustrated book on the history of Pondicherry intended for the general public. This book, so long in the writing, is now before you thanks to all.

My special thanks to:
The Department of Art and Culture, Government of Pondicherry; the Department of Art and Culture, Government of Tamil Nadu; the Department of Tourism, Government of Pondicherry; le Centre des Archives d'Outre-Mer, Aix-en-Provence; l'École Française d'Extrême-Orient, Pondicherry; Fort Saint George Museum, Chennai; Hôtel de l'Orient, Pondicherry; the Indian National Trust for Art and Cultural Heritage, Pondicherry; l'Institut Français de Pondichéry; la Réunion des Musée Nationaux, Paris; Sri Aurobindo Ashram Library, Pondicherry; le Lycée français de Pondichéry; le Musée de la Compagnie des Indes, Lorient; the Museum of Pondicherry; the National Library of Australia; Romain Rolland Library, Pondicherry; Sri Aurobindo Ashram Trust, Pondicherry; Vatika Guest Home and Boutique; Versailles Curios, Pondicherry.

Acknowledgements

And also to:
Jean Deloche for his counsel and encouragement; late Ajit Koujalgi and Ashok Panda of INTACH for supporting the project; late Joseph Goubert for putting his collection at my disposal; Rangaswami for throwing his house open to me; Peter Heehs for guiding me in the Ashram Archives; Ganesh Bala for letting me make use of illustrations that appeared in *Realty*; late Francis Warcziag for putting his collection at my disposal; Shaupon Bose for his useful comments; Cristof Pitoëf for proofreading of the French version; Maurice Shukla, Sunaina Panda and Virginia Soukup for the English translation; the entire team of INTACH-Pondicherry for making appointments, executing drawings and supporting the author and particularly Naveem Akkina, Sivaram Prasad and S. Vaigai; Kota Noble from Romain Rolland Library; Elizabeth de Farcy for her interest; Christopher Tyack for his revision; late Robi Ganguli for his advice on design and last but not least, Jacqueline Charbonnier and Datta Mukherjee for their constant work, help and patience.

Photo Credits

Centre des Archives d'Outre-Mer, Aix-en-Provence: 27 (©CAOM); 42 (©CAOM); 44-45 (©CAOM); back cover. **Sebastian Cortes:** 35b (©S.C.). **EFEO, Pondicherry:** 4-5 (©EFEO); 25 (©EFEO); 91 (©EFEO). **IFP:** 46b (©IFP-EFEO); 127 (©IFP-EFEO); 139c (©IFP-EFEO). **INTACH-Pondicherry:** 28; 33; 40; 79, 80-81; 114-115; 148-149; 149. **INTACH-Pondicherry/ Joseph Goubert:** 58b; 109a; 119; 122-123; 142. **Koujalgi Ajit:** 9c; 13; 24a; 36-37; 46a; 49; 50; 50-51; 57; 59b; 61; 62-63; 68a; 82-83; 95; 96-97; 98-99; 105; 106; 110-111; 116; 118; 121; 125. **Malangin Raphaël:** 30-31 (with kind permission of Sri Aurobindo Library); 64; 65b; 84c; 90a-c; 94; 96; 109b-g; 112; 130. **Malangin Raphaël/Pondicherry Museum:** 6a; 6c; 16; 17; 22; 24; 32; 35a; 43b; 47; 51; 53b-c; 59; 65a; 69c; 73; 74a-d; 75a-d; 78; 81; 84b; 87; 102a-b; 103; 104; 109h. **Molinari Giorgio/Collection Francis Wacziarg:** 8; 9a; 21a; 22; 26; 38; 39; 43a; 46c; 72; 84a; 134a-b; 135b-c; 143; 151; 153. **Musée de la Compagnie des Indes, Lorient:** 13 (©Musée de la Compagnie des Indes, Lorient); 14 (© Yvon Boëlle); 15 (©Musée de la Compagnie des Indes, Lorient); 19 (© Yvon Boëlle/Musée de la Compagnie des Indes, Lorient); 21b (© Yvon Boëlle); 21c (© Yvon Boëlle/Musée de la Compagnie des Indes, Lorient). **Réunion des Musées Nationaux, Paris:** 12 (©RMN/Château de Versailles)/Gérard Blot; 88 (©RMN/droits réservés); 100 (©RMN/ Musée d'Orsay)/Hervé Lewandowski. **National Library of Australia:** 66-67 (©National Library of Australia); 69b (©National Library of Australia); 71 (©National Library of Australia); 74-75 (©National Library of Australia); 76 (©National Library of Australia); 86 (©National Library of Australia). **Robi Ganguli/Collection Francis Wacziarg:** 56. **Romain Rolland Library:** 6b; 9b; 18a-d; 20; 41a-b; 52a-c; 53; 54a-b; 55; 58; 68; 69a; 92-93; 120a-d; 134c; 135a; 138; 139a; 145a. **Sri Aurobindo Ashram:** 126; 131; 139b. **Vidyavrata:** 128-129; 132-133; 136-137; 140-141; 144 (attributed to); 145b (attributed to); 154-155; 156.

* Pictures are identified from top to bottom and from left to right of the page. Despite our best efforts, we were unable to contact some copyright-beneficiaries of old documents whose reproductions have been used here. We thank them, nevertheless, for their involuntary participation in this project.

Right: Brahmin wife,
lithograph, late 18th century.

ISBN: 978-81-7436-986-4

Published in India by Roli Books
M-75, Greater Kailash - II Market
New Delhi - 110 048, India
Phone: ++91-11-4068 2000
Fax: ++91-11-2921 7185
Email: info@rolibooks.com
Website: www.rolibooks.com

Editor: Neelam Narula
English translation: Sunaina Panda and Maurice Shukla
Critical editing: Virginia Soukup
Proof reading: Cristof Pitoëff
Layout: Raphaël Malangin; Jean-Denis Ardoin; Kumar
Production: Shaji Sahadevan

Printed and bound in Rave India

Dedicated to Conservation

Join INTACH:

Serve India by protecting its heritage

•

Preserve the heritage of your locality and state

•

Become an active member of INTACH chapter in your region

•

Support INTACH's conservation movement

•

ABOUT INTACH

The Indian National Trust for Art and Cultural Heritage (INTACH) is India's largest non-profit membership-based organization dedicated to conservation and preservation of India's natural, cultural, living, tangible, and intangible heritage. Its mission is to:

- Sensitize the public about the pluralistic cultural legacy of India;
- Protect and conserve our living, built, and natural heritage by undertaking necessary actions and measures;
- Document unprotected buildings of archaeological, architectural, historical and aesthetic significance; and cultural resources, as this is the first step towards formulating conservation plans;
- Develop heritage policy and regulations, and make legal interventions to protect our heritage when necessary;
- Provide expertise in the field of conservation, restoration and preservation of specific works of art; and encourage capacity building by developing skills through training programmes

INTACH Pondicherry Chapter is dedicated to preserving the architectural heritage and improving the urban environment of the former French colonial city of Pondicherry on the East Coast of India. Please visit: www.intachpondicherry.org / www.intach.org